PRAISE FOR *The Magician*

THE MAGICIAN'S DAUGHTER—A MEMOIR is a unique memoir and coming-of-age story by author and former journalist Katy Grabel. Reading this book, I experienced the heady delight of imagination in a young girl, fueled by her ever-optimistic father. I also identified with a more universal feminine perspective, that of those of us entranced by the soaring ambitions of a lover, spouse, or—as in this case—a father, and the cognitive and emotional dissonance once that holy grail of desired dreams tips over. There is so much love in this tale of father and daughter, bittersweet and yet deep, and in the end, there is still a joy— of the shared hopes and journeys into unknown vistas via the unreliable contraptions of life. Katy waves her own magic wand, that of the pen, delicate and intricate, lacy and evocative of the illuminated manuscript of her girlhood journal, belying truth, beauty, and humor. Not every-thing in life is as we wish, but if we believe enough, we can still wing our way into a magic kingdom and see what mysteries await us. I know one thing: I'm riding with Katy and her parents.

~Andrea Foster, also known as The Booklady, founder of Creative Quills, author, marketing and publishing pro, and catalyst for change.

A MARVELOUS COMING-OF-AGE STORY . . . the greatest magic happens not on stage or behind the curtains but within the human heart.

~Ann Marie Jackson, author of *The Broken Hummingbird*.

KATY GRABEL'S FINELY DETAILED account describes the last performances of the Broadway Magical Mystery Extravaganza, her illusionist father's magic show. Captivating and well-written, the story has wonderful momentum and expands a poignant, handmade moment just before the onset of broadcast monotainment. Her observations peek into the heart of a man who could make something out of nothing and the effects of his dreams on her own heart.

~Carol Terry, author of *Where We Live: Notes on Navigating the Absolute* and *Greening the Blues: Healing Patterns of Grief*.

MEMOIRS ARE INTRIGUING—WE WONDER how the writer, now seemingly past the events of a younger or different self, gets through their life. Grabel begins her memoir as an adolescent, living a 1950s suburban life: Swimming pool, green grass, mother cooking, father walking out the door dressed in suit and tie and briefcase—but like so many familiar family scenes, we know there is a secret: the father is a magician. That is a performer of illusion. We know this in the memoir's title. Still, there is a journey to be taken that will break into the frames of illusion, both the "magic tricks" and the family relations, and, of course, how Grabel finds her own magic. In this classic tale, this journey reveals the strengths and weaknesses of each person, as well as glimpses of the framework and artistry of the illusions themselves. So for the performance, and so for the family dynamics. A journey of revelations!

This is a unique memoir. The adult Grabel looks back at herself, her family, the many characters the journey brings, and, most of all, the young woman she is becoming. Bring your own magic into this book. Read it.

–Veronica Golos, author of *GIRL*.

THE MAGICIAN'S DAUGHTER TAKES us on a unique journey into the hidden realm of the magician's hat to discover its dark secrets. Lots of ABRACADABRA moments!

–Sandra Richardson, award-winning author of *Splinters*.

The MAGICIAN'S Daughter

Cover Photo: Anca Asmarandei/EyeEm
Cover Design: John LaSala/gluedesign.com

Editor: Judyth Hill
Book Design: Mary Meade
www.wildrisingpress.com

First Edition
ISBN 978-1-957468-37-2

The MAGICIAN'S *Daughter*

a memoir

KATY GRABEL

Wild Rising Press

EVERGREEN, COLORADO

With love and gratitude
to my parents

It's still magic even if you know how it's done.

—Terry Pratchett, *Hatful of Sky*

❧

The house of magic has many rooms.

—Eugene Burger

❧

I feel like I should capture this time in my life and put it in a plastic container or something. Keep it. Because I know some day I'm going to want it back.

—Katy's journal

Backstage, I walked through a patchwork of light and dark, past equipment draped as silent beings in half light. Shadows fell in angular blocks from wall to floor, then opened to dimly lit areas, then fell to darkness again. A makeshift twilight. A half-toned Disneyland. A magic show in those quiet pre-show hours is like a big dusty attic above a long-suffering world, filled with old devotions and charms everyone forgot were there.

PROLOGUE

I LOVED THE WAY the words "Las Vegas" felt in my body, like a gush of hot, throaty wind. I wanted to be the fond sidekick of showgirls, a showbiz kid, the girl who jumped out of a big top hat in her father's magic show, a kind of celebrity. To my father, Las Vegas was the mecca for professional magicians. A big casino stage had all the amenities for a magician to show his stuff. A magician like him, who had to make up for lost time—time behind a desk, and time getting older—for the seventeen years his show was in storage. A magician who was very good, just not very famous.

We had only been on the road four days when kingly destiny took hold. My father's scorching blue eyes held me in his gaze as he explained the particulars of a Vegas stage. "Traps right in front, and a mirror tunnel for the big cats." His breath was as fast as a bird's that must fly in place. "Striplights, footlights, floodlights, and spots. They have lights that can look like the moon."

We were in a motel room in Ukiah sitting across from each other on two beds, somewhere between a glorious new life and our old one. Nodding my head, I imagined that brilliant stage with him in the center of it, arms open to receive the applause as he finally redeemed himself from all those boring Chamber of Commerce mixers back home.

In the artificial light, his white hair exuded a royal pewter gleam. It had turned white early in his life, making him appear much older than he really was. His receding hairline displayed the curve of his skull and an overexposed pink face. My father's forehead was particularly high, cheeks very grainy, nose too tender.

Behind him, my mother napped with a *Good Housekeeping* magazine open across her chest, her pretty face cast in slumber. How could she sleep with such big plans underway? Dad and I had our feet on the floor, ready for action, whether it be friend or foe or casino executive with a contract in hand.

"Artistic control, that's what we want. If not, we're doing *The Zig Zag* till kingdom come," he cautioned. "Multi-year contract, two, five years, a good solid booking." He had that same far-off gaze I had seen at tee-off when his ball cleared the sand traps.

I squirmed in my seat, too excited to keep still. The cinema of my imagination started to roll, frame after frame. I, as his assistant, cast in unearthly white light, a thousand eyes watching me onstage. Nothing would be finer than a Vegas booking: red-velvet dressing rooms, slick jeweled stages, and the kind of applause I could feel on my skin. I softly smiled. For this tour, I'd been taken out of the eighth grade, and now everything smacked of destiny.

I lifted my head as he stood up. For all his touted marvels, knot escapes, and big animal productions, he wore average dress—trousers, thin leather belt, mustard golf shirt. The only exception was his smart, thick-heeled ankle boots.

"You know what they say about Vegas magicians?" he asked, his eyebrows floating up and a puckish grin dancing around the corners of his mouth. "They're all top hat. No rabbit."

This talk of Vegas had turned him uncharacteristically jolly, and we exchanged reckless grins. Before this, he'd been another kind of father, always busy, absent, preoccupied elsewhere. He was a near-stranger to me. A man with a briefcase walking out our front door or wading into our pool on winter mornings, so obscured by drifts of steam he was only an impression of a man lost in mist. He'd had simple desires back then. *I'll have the king salmon, no sauce, just lemon; pretend I'm a monk.* And now he and I were united by this adventure, conferring and planning. I stopped. Blinked. Something about this didn't feel right. How would our four-month tour of one-nighters land us Vegas? We played modest towns with modest stages. A far leap from big, glitzy Vegas.

Just then, I heard a clink. Dad tossed a silver coin into the air, a big moon-faced coin of muted silver. Houdini's rent money unblessed by God and commerce. It spun and whirled and almost touched the ceiling before dropping into his open palm. The coin was from his routine, and he bought them by the dozens to replace the ones he lost onstage.

He leaned in close to me, his hair a sweeping drift of snow. As he rubbed his fingers for bounty, a second coin appeared in the lamplight, trembling between his fingers. His eyes narrowed. "Of course, to get that Vegas booking, the right people have to see the show," he said solemnly.

"Who?" I asked, eager to know.

"The talent scouts from the casinos," he explained. "The Sahara, the Stardust, the Sands…They're all going to be at the Las Vegas show."

Our small tour included one night with the Kiwanis Club of Las Vegas at the convention center behind the strip. My breath caught. *Of course.* He had intentionally booked that show because of its proximity to the clubs. It would be easy for the casino executives to slip into their big black sedans and attend our show. *That* was how this tour could get us a casino booking. We were scheduled to appear May 9th, toward the end of our travels, almost four months away.

We had one show to impress those casino talent scouts.

I imagined our crew standing primly onstage with their hands behind their backs, a hocus-pocus squad in shiny shoes and rhinestones, pouncing at their cues, as nimble as trained black cats. I felt a twitch of fear and didn't know why. On the bed, Mom's eyelids fluttered with internal chatter. Through the window, I spotted, parked in a corner of the motel lot, the truck that carried our show's equipment. It was drizzling, and the white trailer looked like a big, moist, snowy mountain about to slide away in an avalanche.

I have the same wide, roomy forehead as my father, and the same thin, flower-petal eyelids. When I turn my face just so, our profiles are similar—delicate and softly sloping, trustful in the direction we are facing. My father and I were doomed. As madly as my heart beat in that motel room, it was the heart of a traitor. At our one show in Las Vegas, I would betray my father's biggest dream.

CONTENTS

THE GREAT HOUDINI UP IN THE SKY

RIGHT PLACE AT THE RIGHT TIME—EXACTLY

GRABEL SHOW
CAPACITY CROWDS... AND FILLED AUDITORIUMS ACROSS THE NATION
LEE
GRABEL
starring
Helene
and the FAMOUS
FLOATING PIANO

I

THE LOPSIDED HOUSE

What a life. A warehouse full of illusions and one pair of pants.

—WILLARD THE WIZARD

1

⌒⌒⌒

THE STRANDED MAGIC SHOW

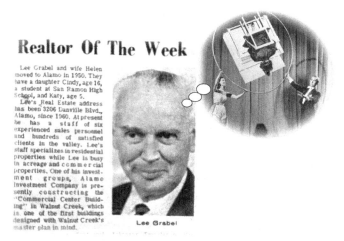

Realtor Of The Week

Lee Grabel and wife Helen
moved to Alamo in 1950. They
have a daughter Cindy, age 16,
a student at San Ramon High
School, and Katy, age 5.
Lee's Real Estate address
has been 3206 Danville Blvd.,
Alamo, since 1960. At present
he has a staff of six
experienced sales personnel
and hundreds of satisfied
clients in the valley. Lee's
staff specializes in residential
properties while Lee is busy
in acreage and commercial
properties. One of his investment groups, Alamo
Investment Company is pre-
sently constructing the
"Commercial Center Build-
ing" in Walnut Creek, which
is one of the first buildings
designed with Walnut Creek's
master plan in mind.

Lee Grabel

The Valley Pioneer, 1967

As THE DAUGHTER OF a great magician, I learned:

~ Never play Crazy Eights with his manipulation deck.

~ When buying shoes for the show, always get an extra pair for the
dummy—about a size five.

~ Ten-pound fish line is good for more than catching trout.

~ "Did he saw your mother in half?" is a question folks often ask
me, to which I respond, "No, he wanted to be original. He
sawed her vertically."

~ Magic is never where I think it will be.

My schooling as the daughter of a magician didn't begin until I was
fourteen years old, in 1977. That was when my father launched a
magnificent comeback to professional magic. In the fifties, my parents

trekked from desert to bayou in their big chrome-lit illusion show, featuring The Floating Piano, a real spinet played upside down by a slew of piano teachers, one from every stop on tour. Despite the crowds that flocked to see it, the show was on the verge of extinction. Slowly, their audiences were being ambushed by RCA color-console television sets.

By 1958, my parent's route was decimated, and they settled in Alamo, California, a suburb of San Francisco. I was born shortly thereafter in 1962. They opened a real estate office. Dad sold houses, and Mom typed listings at her secretary's desk. We lived in the rhythm of work and school, and I could almost believe we were an average family except—I was growing up in the flotsam of a ship-wrecked magic show.

Hanging in the back of Mom's closet were old bathing suits edged in twinkling rhinestones, suggesting the cabana wear of lounging showgirls. Tucked next to the freezer in the garage was an old wire dove cage, still lined at the bottom with auto-club road maps. In the kitchen hutch was a true-to-life ceramic egg, except for a piece of red silk sticking out of a little hole. A white-and-red-speckled Bee deck from my father's old card routine was stowed in the drawer of his bed-side table. There were at least seventy cards with a smattering of thin white lines bound many times by a rubber band. And more cards in their jackets, marked by his black scribble, a personal code denoting their degree of elasticity. Stored in our garage was the equipment— old dark-green crates stacked up to the rafters, like a shabby rookery of ravens. There were so many of them, our four-car garage couldn't fit a single car.

Lying on a shelf in the spare bedroom was a big scrapbook jammed with newspaper clippings from their show years. I loved opening the tattered navy-blue cover and studying the far-flung mast-heads and dark, grainy photos of the upright ivory piano suspended midair, my father a dark blotch except for a fleshy hand reaching out. The *Vicksburg Herald* had called him "one of the world's greatest illu-sionists." The *Bismarck Tribune* had referred to him as "world-famous for his unbelievable feats." The *El Reno Daily Tribune* had written, "Grabel's magical showmanship is startling." Turning the scrapbook's big pulpy pages, I read about "standing-room-only crowds," "capacity crowds," "spellbound crowds," "sellouts," and "full houses."

Most interesting of all was the big box of old photographs stashed in the closet. Occasionally, I would riffle through those silver-toned glossies and photos, my father in silky black tails encased in shattering white light, and my mother's supine form in drowsy slumber, mid-air in a gossamer gown. As fascinated as I was, my casual foray into that box always squeezed the air out of me—I had missed something grand. There were photos of seated crowds with sunny smiles, gas stations blanketed in snow, and a large truck with The Lee Grabel Show splashed on the sides. And more photos of a dazzling cannon barrel trimmed in cut mirror, a spiffy beach-tanned crew seated around a big gold top hat, and my parents bowing and holding hands, looking leggy and fine. For hours I'd sift through those photos, each more intriguing than the last, each slipping out of my hands like all that lost magic...gone, gone.

I would always pause on a photo of my older sister, Cindy, at age five, in a red-checkered jumper, posing on a box with my glamorous young parents. Each time I saw that photo I fell into a little dark hole. My mother had given birth to Cindy on the road, and my sister had traveled and performed in their incredible show. Holding the photo by its white trim, the unfairness of it always felt so unbearable. Cindy, eleven years older than me, had moved out of the house when I was six. She lived in the area and worked as a secretary.

The house was very quiet without her. On many afternoons I would hear our lawn sprinklers and the cries of kids playing down the street, and think about those photos of the magic show. Alamo was nice—and so boring, next to the show's enchantments. Each time I inspected those photos it was hard to draw myself away. I would keep looking, photo after photo, hoping my own image would finally surface.

Oh, here I am.

"Why were you a magician?" I asked Dad one morning as he threw back his coffee.

He wasn't a big man, just medium sized, and he might have been overlooked in a crowd except for his fast, purposeful gait in his pursuit of anything from a butter pecan ice cream cone to a listing on a four-bedroom house. He had to be the only man in the world who vibrated when standing still.

"That was how we made a living back then," he answered and straightened his tie knot.

He rarely indulged my curiosity about the magic show. *Oh, honey, shooting your mom from the cannon paid the bills. If only I could have landed that dream job selling life insurance.* In truth, I think his years as a businessman had made him a little embarrassed of his former love. He had come to realize just how distrustful mainstream America was of a traveling magician. This was probably why he cultivated a reputation as a fair businessman, even adding the word "Integrity" below his name on his business cards. What's more, he believed many magicians weren't very good, and he was always setting himself apart from the worst of his brethren—those feeble rank-and-file weekend magicians who played kiddie parties, middling nightclubs, or spiritless fraternal halls with a show they could fit in the back of their cars. He, on the other hand, believed he had belonged to a superior breed of conjurer, one with a monied route, big illusions, and a deft crew. His desire had been too pure, his labor too godly, and his showmanship too fine to be compared with most magicians.

"We played one-nighters over the lower forty-eight, nine months a year, for thirteen years," he said with a hint of pride in his voice. He attributed his success in building his show equipment from sappy pine and molten glass to his tireless American work ethic. Even JP Morgan, leader of the Industrial Age, would have been impressed. Dad tugged on the white cuffs of his sleeves. "I drove so much, almost shot out the nerves in my gas-pedal leg."

From the kitchen table Mom added, "Honey, it was a lot of hard work, but I did get pancakes at midnight." She was assembling party favors for my eleventh birthday party, chin tucked, hands flying. "What about this for your friends?" she asked, holding up a puka-shell necklace.

I eyed Dad's nicked and scratched cowhide briefcase. "Can't you do a show around here?"

He tucked his yellow paper to-do list inside his suit jacket and pushed up his black, thick-rimmed glasses. "Oh, no. I need a truck to haul it, a sit-down audience, a follow spot, at least five assistants, and a fifteen-minute intermission to rest." He appeared to be checking off items on a clipboard. "It was a Big Show." *The Big Show.* That's what he called it. He'd say, "Back with the Big Show," or "That was when we had the Big Show."

He picked up his briefcase and ran his hand across his untainted ivory hair. Although he preferred it ungelled and unbarbered, it was often shaggy around the ears, as he was too busy for regular haircuts. He glanced at his wristwatch. On Tuesdays, he gave pep talks to his sales staff. "The Big Show is a thing of the past," he said with finality.

Yet he still had those old cards stashed in his bedside table.

A question formed in my belly, whimpered for air, words aligning into a sentence. Poking out from his wool trouser hems were the buffed alligator shoes that would soon march him back to his office desk stacked with paper, a ringing phone, and a big Multiple Listings Service book.

"Can you do a show at my party?" I blurted out.

His pink face drained of color, and the breath left his body. In a voice thick with false apology, he explained to me what kind of magic he did not do. "Oh, honey, I don't do shows for kids."

From her pile of invitations, ribbons, and balloons, Mom said in her best shame-on-you voice, "Lee!"

He squeezed his eyes shut. I wondered what was so dreadful. I just wanted to see that lauded old magic come alive, all those photos and headlines unboxed and free. "Okay," he croaked and walked out the door.

For the birthday show, Dad stationed himself in front of our fireplace with the kids on the floor. As soon as he brandished his big silver rings, the little boys turned into a pack of squirming snakes. When he unlinked two big silver rings, they cried, "I see a hole!" When he vanished a card, they exclaimed, "It's behind his hand!" They lunged for his legs and reached for his arms. Mom had to get in the center of the boys and pull them back by their belt loops. Hopping up and down, Dad frantically ruffled and fanned cards in hopes of distracting them.

I twisted birthday ribbon around my fingers, horrified as the disaster unfolded. Finally, he cut the show short, and as the kids cleared out, I slunk behind them. This lackluster display of magic certainly didn't live up to all those old photos and headlines. Later, I figured out why my father always called his show *cosmopolitan*. It was a code word for *a show for adults*. He never wanted to be, nor was he ever, a magician that performed only for children. He didn't own a single trick geared for kids.

After my party, I tried to understand what the abandoned magic show meant—all its strange muted remnants in our drawers and closets, the lost old cargo in our garage, and its unanswered promises my father was unable to release.

"Don't let your friends in the garage," he would tell me. He fretted that the neighborhood boys who knew he was a magician would break in and snoop around. The mere nearness of his show, he believed, would turn those boys into marauding, plundering hoodlums. His fears confounded me. For a magician's garage, it was terribly uninteresting. No hanging string or impaling swords, no fake women's feet. Just bugs, cobwebs, mousetraps, and old wintergreen crates. Still, something in its curious heft preoccupied him. At night, he always locked the garage door before going to bed, and he devised a plan for pumping out pool water in case a housefire ever endangered the garage.

I would lie on my canopy bed, feeling the psychic bulk of those

The Magician's Daughter: A Memoir

25

crates in the garage. Their weight and history pulled our house one way, making it feel lopsided, everything drifting and listing toward the garage. To drop a marble in one room was to discover it by the garage door. Moving from one side of the house to another, all detours and paths led past that door.

The rest of my parents' show was kept in a green trailer next to a horse corral down the road from Lee Grabel Realty. Each Halloween night, just as I donned my costume and grabbed an empty pillowcase for my loot, Dad would head out the door for the trailer. Parked next to its old slumped shape, he guarded it against the same hoodlums plotting burglary of his garage. At the end of the night, as I picked through my candy, he would return in his golf windbreaker with the remains of a sandwich Mom had fixed him.

Meanwhile, he negotiated deals with bankers and scouted golden hillocks to subdivide. When he returned home from work, his briefcase hung loosely from his fingers as if he didn't belong to that world either. "I'm beat," he would gasp, sinking into a living room chair. Mom and I would jump into action. She poured him a beer while I laid the evening newspaper in his lap. He rested his head on the back of the chair, his body completely still and the corners of his white shirt collar turned down into the thumbprints of a ghost. Having left home at a young age, my father knew how to work hard and be resourceful. Being an entertainer packed him with confidence, and he moved through the world with his whole spirit. It exhausted him. The whorl of his actions rippled out into the universe and dumped him in his chair each night, spent and drained.

I wished he would notice me.

After school, I would sit by the front door of the real estate office reading, while down the rows of desks, behind a glass door, Dad talked with a phone under his chin. Sometimes he would reach inside his jacket pocket with the stealth of a Western fast draw and pull out his yellow list, jot something down, and slip it back in. His "yellow list" consisted of pages from a pad of yellow legal-size paper, folded into quarters and held together with a pen clip. Each day he would turn to a new page and write a list in his inky, illegible script: things to do, places to go, people to see. Everything he accomplished started off on a list, and his days were governed by the size of that list.

On short-list days he roamed about the office with hands in pockets, trying to ward off the midday tedium. The salespeople, usually retirees and chain-smoking divorcées, would look up from their MLS books to hear about his early escapades.

"I got so lost—there was La Sonoma and La Serena, Waverly and Wayland," he said, amused by his own hapless wandering. "I'd say to couples in the car, 'Just showing you the neighborhood.'"

Our vaudevillian banter soon followed.

"You want to see my elevator dance?" he asked me, his face bright, unpuckered, a bursting smile of crooked teeth.

"*Soitantly!*" I said.

His feet jumped, arms open. "Ta da! No steps!"

We would bask in our cleverness, flashing our bad teeth at each other. Braces were clamped on my buck teeth, and his incisors slanted in a variety of angles. In promotional photos, he had learned to express mischief in the eyes while keeping his mouth closed. He was the master of a disarming closed-lip smile that curled up at the ends like a frilly line of cake frosting.

"If you were a card, you'd be the joker," I teased.

"Watch out or I'll turn you into a rabbit," he answered.

"Can't you ground me instead?"

Sometimes he danced a sloppy "Shuffle off to Buffalo" next to Mom's desk with the skill of a happy-go-lucky, song and dance man.

Long-list days were more common. Charging in and out of the office, he offered me only the whine of his raw voltage as he passed without a wink or a quip. Even with my behind in the chair and back straight, I felt sheer, permeable, in his wake, just static and shadow against the wall.

"Stress management is for sissies," he was famously known to tell my mother.

One day he noticed me by the office door and said, "What do you know? You're just a little girl." Too rushed to spare   breath between syllables, his words often ran together: *Whatdoyouknowyou'rejustalittlegirl.* He had paused mid-stride, his arms momentarily caught in a maze of wire as he studied me. His furrowed brow and clouded eyes invited none of our playful banter. My gaze dropped to the floor. He smelled of tartar sauce from lunch. I sensed grinding, churning machinery inside him—gears, shafts, and wheels torqued to the limit.

After dinner, he sometimes sat at his desk at home and made calls.

"I met you the other day when you came by my office. I've got some nice homes to show you." His words were slow and robotic.

He kept on dialing. "I'm Lee Grabel. I've heard you're looking for a house."

Sometimes folks hung up on him and he dialed again.

"I'm Lee Grabel, your local realtor."

Some magicians are unremarkable. They close their shows with the weakest trick and bore their audiences with stale patter and bad jokes.

They fail to understand this fundamental principle of professional magic—it's not about fooling people.

Good magicians shun stock illusions and build their own. They rehearse, rehearse, and rehearse. They labor over their patter and jokes with the zeal of a grandmother sewing lace, the featherstitch just so. Such tired tricks as The Egg Bag, Torn and Restored Newspaper, and Zombie are reborn in their hands.

That brings me to the last thing I've learned as a daughter of a magician. A magician separated from his magic show is without peace. He suffers. He lives only for the day he can return as caretaker of his show's downy light and hard-edged miracles. For my father that happened suddenly.

One night our lives changed.

2

SHY GIRL WITH HUGE LONGING

Helen and Katy, wearing her Elton John glasses

HE WAS SHORT, WITH twigs for arms and legs and a grin larger than he was. Long brown hippie hair framed his face and fell down to his shoulders. No tuxedo, no top hat. He wore velvet overalls decorated with glittery moons and stars. His dancing hands cast charms—things blooming, rising, flowing, falling, jumping from them. Bouncing around the stage, he alighted here and there with a wand or a sword.

"Welcome to my world of magic," he said to my father and me through our television screen.

Over on the sofa my mother scratched out her grocery list. "Who's he?" she asked, her gaze briefly lifting up. "Cream, bread, chicken broth, butter…"

Dad remained riveted to the friendly magician in the box of counterfeit light. The date was December 1975, and it was Doug Henning, the first magician to be featured in his own hour-long network special, live on prime-time television. Usually, it was hard for magicians to land television bookings. They played only talk shows, variety shows, or Mark Wilson's *Magic Circus*. This was the night everything changed. Henning's live show would garner six million viewers and turn him into a celebrity, making professional magic hot entertainment again.

My father must have sensed the shift. Sitting in his wingback chair, he tapped his tawny ankle boots on the floor to test the new ground on which he found himself. When Henning produced a celebrity from a Wurlitzer, Dad nodded approvingly. When he escaped a full tank of water hanging upside down, Dad leaned closer to the set. After Henning jumped off a box, the walls fell away and a black-striped tiger pawed the air. "Nice," Dad purred.

Lying on the floor watching the show, I rested my head on my crossed arms and thought about all the magicians my parents knew, old fussy types with a fondness for olive brine in their martinis. This one was different. I glanced at Dad. He cradled his chin with his strong, pale fingers, watching the show in a scholarly way.

Mom murmured, "Toilet paper. It's on sale," and jotted something down on her list.

The show ended. By that time, I suspect, my father had put it together. Magic show. Network TV. Prime time. Millions of viewers. A new age of professional magic had dawned. Many times I have returned to that moment when my father finally awoke from his long sleep in the suburbs. I see his erect spine, hands suddenly with no place to rest, and hear his silent vow to claim the stages of popular entertainment once again.

He then said something that at the time I didn't understand. "Magic's back," he murmured. A summons of sorts from wild twilight, a black cape flapping.

I remember watching his sure-footed exit from the room. *Magic's back.* I wondered what he meant. Magic was in the garage, as always.

My mother tapped her list with the pen. "I can't forget the rosemary." Tomorrow night she was fixing chicken with roasted red potatoes.

~⁀

When my father was a young boy, he ran up to his mother and cried, "Give me something to do with my hands!" I guess the pots and pans she shoved his way weren't what he needed.

He was born Merle Levy Grabeel in 1919 in Portland, Oregon, the first son of Stewart and Grace Grabeel, two uprooted Missourians far from the Ozark backcountry. He didn't know the big families his parents had left behind except for photos showing lanky uncles with high, rippling foreheads and giggling young aunts in paisley dresses. Stewart Grabeel drove a trolley for the city and stood firm and lean in his granite-gray uniform with the big brass buttons.

Thin and wan, with a bad case of asthma, Merle Levy Grabeel lost so many fights with other boys, his glasses were held together with thread and tape. Worse still, he couldn't pronounce his name. A speech impediment prevented him from making the "r" sound, which meant "Merle" came out as "Mull." People would ask, "What's your name, little boy?" and he'd have to curl his tongue around the sound. "Muuuuulll." When he was eight, a magician performed at his school and turned newspaper into confetti. Curious, he went to the library to read magic books.

Merle began learning magic tricks, which irritated his father. "When you gonna give up those toys?" he griped as the cork balls wobbled in Merle's hands. His younger brother would join in, and they both would frisk Merle for his lead coins and shaved cards, and parade his billiard-ball shells around the house. Still, he practiced until his fingers ached and muscle memory took hold, until his left hand could mimic the movements of his right. At the age of eleven, he performed his first show for his Boy Scout troop and then booked himself steadily in public schools around the city.

When he turned sixteen, he insisted on having his nickel braces removed from his teeth and fled Portland without finishing high school. When he got to San Francisco, he rechristened himself Lee Grabel and played in local variety shows and society clubs until World War II started. While stationed in Palm Springs, he met my mother, and they quickly married before he was shipped off to the South Pacific to arrange talent shows for the military bases. Upon his return, my parents toured with a small show, and by the age of thirty he had engineered The Floating Piano. With a few more big illusions, a truck, and a new five-person crew, the Big Show was born, and he called it the Broadway Magical Mystery Extravaganza.

They performed various standards such as The Doll House, Sawing, Substitution Trunk, Floating Lady, Floating Ball, and the big closer, The Cannon. The Cannon was constructed from wire hoops, Naugahyde, glue, and plywood in my mother's parents' garage one summer in Okarche, Oklahoma. He started calling my mother the Human Cannonball, and she brought him plates of berry pie while he worked.

Sometimes, driving in the car at night, the white lines floated off the road and curled into a question mark. The artistry of thread and light, hand and implement, dove and silk. Why was he so enamored? "You married a nut," he would tell my mother as he steered them through the night.

My mother once told me, "Lee was a very good magician." A very good magician, who just wasn't very famous. We were lying on her bed in a patch of sunlight, watching dust motes twinkling in the sun above us. At her words my ears perked up. I was always trying to link my humdrum working-Joe father to the man who entertained multitudes with a gold hoop and flaming red ribbon.

"His timing was off," she added, her voice soft and sleepy from the sun pouring in. "If he'd been born earlier, he would have gone all the way."

Great magicians in grand theaters. I remembered my parents mentioning Howard Thurston and Harry Blackstone Sr. I'd seen an old-time lithograph of Blackstone in formal black tie, cavorting with little red devils, implying a dark, sinister character, even though I heard he had framed a Houdini portrait with a toilet seat and sent it to the escape artist as a prank.

Mom rested her hands on her chest. "No one could make it back then. Even Willard the Wizard had to pack up his tent," she said with a sigh. "Milton Berle was so popular, no one showed up Tuesday nights."

I often forgot my father was a magician. He read the newspaper to catch up on current events, and he patched leaky roofs of his rental properties with a bucket of tar. Before bed, dressed in his green-striped pajamas, he played solitaire with a new, unstoried deck that slipped under his fingertips. He stashed golf clubs in his car trunk and boasted he knew the closing times of all the local driving ranges. He was a worrier, a capitalist, and a Rotarian, a realist in almost everything. For many years his ordinariness was perhaps his biggest illusion to me and my mother, and maybe even to himself.

In the end, his pastimes and conventions would not save him. It was the magic show he loved. He loved it more than simple pleasures, more than the moon and stars, because they only made him feel expendable, while his magic show enlarged him. It lavished his days with purpose and gave him a willful stride.

As a businessman, he did not speak of his former profession to avoid such jokes as "Float into a new home with Lee Grabel" or "Need buyers? Lee Grabel will pull them out of his hat." Yet sometimes he could not resist revealing his lauded past. On remote emerald-green fairways with a fellow golfer, or over intimate dinners with close friends, he would solemnly announce, "I was America's Leading

Magician of the 1950s." When talking about his early life, he used those exact words, as if it were a title. That's how I said it, too. "My father was America's Leading Magician of the 1950s." They always asked his name. "Lee Grabel," I'd say. Their faces would drop. "No, no, don't know that name."

After the Doug Henning show, Mom and I ate bowls of vanilla ice cream swirling in chocolate syrup while she flipped through home furnishing magazines. Her hair was tucked behind one ear as she delved into color accents for the living room.

She pointed. "What about this one?" Burnished wood, brassy lamps, and sage throw pillows lifted off the magazine's glossy pages.

I told her what I always told her. "That's neat," I chirped.

She had kicked off her high heels, and they lay on the floor, her stocking feet up on the table. She still wore her good clothes from that day—a skirt with a slit up the side that showed off her shapely legs, and a silk blouse that clung to her curves. She was older than my friends' mothers, albeit more stylish and better looking. Her hazel eyes were flecked with amber, her coffee-brown hair teased and shaped into perfect dips and swirls. No joke—my mother was a looker, a knockout, a dish. This was very much at odds with her down-home Midwestern roots, which allowed her to bypass the assumptions often made about pretty women. She sang along with me to pop songs on the car radio, knelt in the dirt to plant tomatoes each spring, and then sloshed around in the mud to water them. She could roll up her sleeves, sip a beer in a water glass, and prepare a Chateaubriand dinner for two dozen old show folks, no problem.

After we finished our ice cream, we scraped our spoons around the empty bowls and moved on to finding new upholstery for the sofa. She laid a ring of fabric samples on her lap and we studied each swath. Rubbing one between her red fingernails, she positioned it in the lamplight and scrunched up her face.

"Hmmm, maybe," she said, touching her chin, completely absorbed by her home beautification project. My mother was as suited to our life in the suburbs as gravy on a homemade biscuit.

All the razzmatazz of the magic show never really made sense to her. Here in Alamo, her deepest longing for home had finally been satisfied. Her mother's quilts lay on our beds, and cookbooks lined the shelves. In some deep, sensible place inside her, this life had meaning. Tucked into a side pocket of her purse she kept a grocery list—toothpaste, graham crackers, ground chuck—her tidy blue cursive as even and unbroken as sea waves.

I examined the fabric samples on her lap. Her excitement about texture and color and finding the perfect accent table and ottoman for the alcove baffled me. I was a girl with fancy ideas and secret quests, a girl who had decided that life was too serious for domestic campaigns. Before I went to bed, I leaned in for a kiss, and I could see a small dab of chocolate in the corner of her firecracker lips. She smelled of parsley and perfume. We both had been thrilled to find that yellow-flowered canopy for my bed, yet the paternal vibe at home had won me over.

⁓

I wanted to be famous. This was my dream, the only dream, and it filled a shady, mysterious recess of my heart. I was not a girl unloved. I just hated being me. I yearned to be a fancy sort of girl. A smash, winner, hoot, marvel, stunner...I wanted flattery. Nothing could quench that desire, although I came close. In my bedroom at the end of the hall, I came very close.

There, in an ordained corner of the room, my black Jensen record player reigned supreme amid my stacked, scratched records. It had a thin bouncy stylus arm and inset speakers that distorted sound when I turned it up high. Romping bullish guitars, pounding drums. I never got enough. Singing into my pink hairbrush microphone, I gallivanted, spun, gyrated, strutted, spread my arms wide to soak up my applause at the Hollywood Bowl.

People were always watching me in my dresser mirror. I felt them there, an invisible crowd enthralled by the songs I sang to them. They included strangers, teachers, neighbors, relatives, and kids from my junior high. I would crank the volume, feeling their fawning, ubiquitous presence. In every mirror they watched me. I couldn't pass one without primping and posing for them. I wanted the spotlight, the same blue-white blaze that had consumed my father in those photos. I wanted a scrapbook filled with clippings about me and my "standing-room-only crowds," "capacity crowds," "spellbound crowds," "sellouts," and "full houses." I wanted my father to see me, who I really was, and not the one quietly nibbling her cinnamon toast each morning as he gulped his coffee before hurrying out the door.

A great talent lay within me. I was so sure of this that one day, in sixth grade, while hanging out with a few neighborhood girls, I felt a burst of bravado when my favorite song came on the radio. As my bedroom antics unfolded across the lawn with high-steppin' glee—"B-B-B-Benny and the Jets"—it's quite possible I took myself too seriously. Their smiles and laughter, I assumed, were kindly, until they joined in, prancing around. "B-B-B-Benny and the Jets!" they howled. My hopes transmuted into something sad. Could I not be that fabulous? The stamp of hot shame stung. After that I restricted my romping to my bedroom, and my wonderful secret unfolded within its four smooth corners.

That night after the Henning show, I leaped up the stairs to my bedroom for my usual routine—the raucous music, cheering fans, my delirious dancing and singing. Then I studied album photos of my favorite singers. I paused on Elton John in his flamboyant spangled suit and dapper hat, with his big glasses. And Elton sitting at his piano in a feather jumpsuit.

That's what I wanted. To be part beloved showman and part outlandish rock star. Desire hit me hard and etched its name on my tingling skin. Just then, a reporter from *Rolling Stone* magazine materialized at my side with a notepad and a pencil. I crossed my legs with a lady's propriety, touched my chin, and explained my start in the record business.

I left Alamo and I never came back.

I had a few gripes about my hometown. First of all, I believed I'd been unfairly teased. I had inherited my father's speech impediment, which made me susceptible to the usual playground flak. Unable to pronounce *r*, I turned classmates Richard and Rebecca into Wichad and Wobecca. Even my name got mangled by my uncooperative tongue: Katy Gwabel. Visits to a speech therapist in the third grade corrected it, except in my mind I was still Katy Gwabel.

As the only child at home, I didn't have much social confidence with other kids. I ended up chumming around with my parents to fancy white-tablecloth restaurants or going on shopping excursions with my mother. These adult pastimes turned me into an oddball to other girls: I was quick with restaurant recommendations ("Their rack of lamb is superb!") or my mother's home decoration tips ("Bring the outdoors indoors with plants and green pillows!"). I pretended not to notice the funny looks other kids gave me. As a daughter of a popular showman, my uncelebrated status perplexed me. Redemption was always on my mind.

After a while, my feverish fantasizing and lip-syncing divided me into two girls: the girl in my bedroom and the girl who walked out. Outside was Katy Gwabel, a shy, slumpy girl with a mouth of wire and gobs of makeup on her face to conceal her acne. At the mall with other girls, Katy Gwabel was always there, telling her father's silly jokes and trying to impress them with her record collection. I couldn't stand her. Her voice trembled during book presentations at school. She was too timid to sign up for choir.

These feelings confused me and made my big dreams feel unattainable. I believed such things should be as easy as finding magic inside a drawer or crate or closet.

Back at my bedroom mirror, I tried to blot out my pixie face, flanked by a limp, uninspiring Dorothy Hamill haircut. I was thirteen years old, with bad posture and a serious overbite, my first bra digging painfully into my ribs and shoulders, a big sanitary napkin bunched up between my legs. I was new to my junior high and didn't have many friends. I hated the kids who ignored me, and ignored the ones who were friendly, because I thought I was better.

I turned the volume knob of my record player higher, to negate how bad I felt. Tilting my head in the mirror, I let the contours of my face reconfigure into something frisky and sly. I then practiced The Look. I'd seen my father do The Look in numerous family photos. He would disengage from the camera lens and gaze away, cheekbones flared, as if transported beyond the earthly plane. Perhaps it was a theatrical pose he couldn't let go of. Before my mirror, I moved my ears back and, just slightly, my cheekbones lifted. The Look also demanded a certain attitude. Serene exultation. I softened my eyes.

Sometimes, my father did The Look when he thought no one was around. Once, walking down the hall to my bathroom, I glanced into a wall mirror that afforded me a peek into my parents' bedroom. He stood in front of his mirror, head turned, holding that gaze I knew so well. The Look. Different, though. A fantasy played out. He spoke softly into the mirror, his bright blue eyes holding steady as he captured long sideways glances at his reflection. Apparently, he spoke to no one, but I knew that wasn't so.

My father also had invisible crowds. We both yearned for the accolades of strangers. I think of this, years later, and shudder. Every brilliant dream has its casualties—folks who get stuck, lost, or worse, give up.

3

THE RELUCTANT HUMAN CANNONBALL

The Human Cannonball, 1950s

"YOU'RE SERIOUS?" MY MOTHER kept moving, sink to refrigerator to stove, while the agitation on her face told me her mind was far from cooking dinner. She was stuck on what my father had just said. His words filled the kitchen as he repeated himself.

"We must go back," he urged her. "It's time."

He stood at the kitchen counter in his banker's suit with chin held high, ready to captain her into a new life.

She flipped a pork chop. "Hmmp."

I removed the utensils from the drawer—three forks, three knives, three spoons. My thoughts were flying faster than my hands. All I could see was that old slate-tone photo of the show truck, rolling off the celluloid paper and pulling up to our house.

Dad walked to the glass doors and studied our pool, laden with winter leaves, sunken branches, and drowned pinecones. He said, lightly, "We do one tour to get the show in shape, get some publicity going." Stuffing his hands in his pockets, he glanced back at Mom to draw her back to his side, where she had always been. "We'll get the interest of big-time venues."

With avocados sliced, russets mashed, purple onions stirred in with the peppered chops, Mom rummaged through the refrigerator for a stick of butter, as if that, and only that, would deflect this crisis. She fired off a round of questions.

"What about the rental properties?"

"I'll handle it by phone."

"The office?"

"I'll bring in a partner."

"Lee, I'm fifty."

"You look great."

His answers were so fast he must have anticipated her questions. She stopped in the middle of the kitchen and looked at him coolly, her smooth features pointy as darts. She didn't believe him but didn't quite know why.

For so long, the magic show had lived in a diffused, scattered state in our house: a photo here, a gesture, story, or stray prop there. With Dad's announcement I could feel it congealing into one thing, pulling together its lost pieces, including me, into its mysterious squat bulk while my mother was somewhere outside of it, unwilling to step in.

I clamped my jaw. She was going to destroy my big chance to be onstage. The crazed joy that had lifted me up sent me crashing. She must agree. We couldn't do it without her. She carried out the trash and mowed the lawn. She paid the bills and balanced the checkbook in *pen*. One time, she'd fed Dad's entire Masonic lodge a meatloaf dinner with only three hours' notice. Without her, a table for three someplace would be empty.

"I don't know," she said, shaking her head. "I just don't." She wiped her hands on a dishtowel. "We could not possibly. At *this* point in our lives. *Really*."

He then used her show name. "Come on, *Helene*," he said quietly. "It's time to get out there again." In that second, something passed between my parents. Perhaps a memory of lonely byways, woebegone stages, and dancing lights, edged in darkness.

Reaching into his jacket, he pulled out his yellow list and unclipped his pen. "I was thinking, the trailer," he said matter-of-factly. "We need to haul that equipment out, find a place to look things over." He scribbled something. I noted inky black loops, jagged precipices. "And we'll have to inspect the piano. Make sure it's in tip-top shape."

He kept on writing. Items on his list were always happening, always turning from air to palpable things. I froze. Maybe the magic show was being reassembled right in front of me.

My mother must have had the same thought. "Lee!" Her hand flew up to stop this runaway train. "How will we...? What about...?" she asked, breathless.

"We'd have a good booker, a generous cut of the proceeds, and a phone crew to sell tickets," he said with a hint of impatience in his voice. "You saw Henning's show. Magic's popular again." He rubbed his forehead as if all this unnecessary convincing had given him a headache.

Her eyes dulled to gray. As she stroked her throat, I could feel words stalled there. She turned up her nose in defiance. In the pans, pots, and bowls, she quickly dispersed the serving utensils. She stuck a plastic prong in the salad, stuffed a big spoon inside the mashed potatoes, slapped a spatula on the pork chops, and poked a fork in the steamed broccoli.

"Dinner's ready," she said.

⁓

My mother never wanted to be the Human Cannonball. She wanted to be a mom, aunt, sister, and daughter, to live in a cozy brick house down the street from her mother and her sisters, Kate, Ruth Ann, and Minnie Mae. Instead, along their tour of Middle America from Las Cruces to Kansas City to Chattanooga, my father launched her from a cannon. A John Philip Sousa military march blared from the speakers as she was loaded feet first into the barrel, her arms pointing north.

"Good luck on your journey!" my father would call out just before the blast. At that moment, I imagine her wondering what her sisters were doing, hundreds of miles away, maybe coaxing their kids into pajamas and out to kiss their dads goodnight. She imagined looking into their homes from the street, through the curtains into the warm yellow light. Even in her flight jacket and fishnet stockings, she could still smell the red dirt of her childhood on her fingers.

Born Helen Foster in Okarche, Oklahoma, on the flat, wheat-dense prairie, my mother was one of six kids. Her mother's family had owned the hotel in town, and her father was the local entrepreneur, which meant whatever Okarche needed, he provided. He was a barber, pool hall and cafe owner, and mung bean farmer. During World

War II, her family temporarily moved to Palm Springs, California, to be near her two brothers who were stationed at a military base nearby. She worked at the local library, where she met my father. When he first told her, "I'm a magician," she didn't hear him right. "What instrument do you play?" she asked.

He hadn't won her affection with magic tricks. Even then he refused to diminish his art with little pocket effects. I suspect it was his humor and confidence that attracted her. They quickly married, and he was shipped off overseas. Although she knew he was a magician, she thought of him as a soldier who might die in the war. When he returned alive, she was dismayed to realize she had married a magician.

Ambivalent about the magic show, she remained pragmatic. Being shot from a cannon wasn't that different from mashing potatoes for thirty hungry ranchers. Still, I wonder on what lonely stretch of road she started to say, "How long are we going to do this?" Even when my sister, Cindy, was born, the trouping continued, and Cindy slept in a crib backstage during the show.

After the decline of their magic show, my father insisted on settling in Alamo, where they owned a summer home. My mother appeared to become a Californian even as she told everyone— from neighbors to store cashiers to strangers—that she was from Oklahoma. She would even swipe her fist through the air and sing that line from the musical, "*Oooooooooklahoma...*" It was good to be an Okie. She kept a coffee can of bacon grease next to the saffron in the kitchen, and she preferred ice cubes in her beer. Her father was born in a cave from his half-blood Indian mother, and she didn't know much about her Native American heritage except that it gave her high cheekbones and straight hair that she labored over to get a decent curl.

On visits to the Foster clan, I would watch her bob around, hugging nieces and nephews, and giving her creamy cheek to the men to kiss. She belonged to them, and they to her. I'd never seen her so happy. Only in Oklahoma did I wonder if our trio was too small for her. My aunts and mother had the same lean, sturdy bodies, the same unfaltering command of household domains. To see them cook in the kitchen was to see a symphony of camaraderie and coordination, all of them hurrying around laughing and talking while waving big wooden spoons and spatulas in the air. Frying, flipping, and mashing. Tossing, stirring, and chopping, never once bumping into each other.

During one visit, we met her sisters for lunch at Grandma's house, and eventually the lively conversation drifted to folks Mom didn't know.

"Are those the Coopers that lived on Chisholm?" Mom asked.

No, no, they said. This was another family. They continued chatting while Mom sat silently. On and on they talked about events that occurred long after Mom had moved away. I glanced at her. She turned away to hide her tears.

"Come on, let's take these dishes in," she said, standing up.

She could never regain those years apart, and she never had close women friends to replace her sisters. There was a reason she named me Katherine after her big sister and Ruth after her mother and little sister. I must have sensed from an early age she needed me to step in for her missing family. Still, much of what ailed her was beyond a child's remedy.

My father had the "Big Show," while Mom had "home." She would say, "I gotta call home," or "I wonder how everyone is at home." Home. And she said it from an exhalation deep within, short and fast, unable to linger long on the word. While my father watched over the trailer on Halloween and protected his garage from neighborhood delinquents, my mother was planting her aunt's Easter lily bulbs, and her mother's adored rose, Joseph's Coat. She noted her father's favorite pie, cherry, in every restaurant pie display she passed. She dreamed of flat expanses of red dirt and the Sunday suppers she missed with the family, clanking their spoons against their iced tea glasses. Shopping for furniture, we would walk through cavernous warehouses full of empty living room displays. Often we were the only people in these huge stores, and sometimes I would run ahead to scout things out. Looking back, I would see her walking down the aisle from a distance, a miniature Mom soldiering through vacant rooms.

In the old cannon photo, my mother posed, ready for flight— half out of the barrel, with a leather skullcap snug on her head. She wore Amelia Earhart wrist-high gloves, her index fingers pointing and her arms shaped into a perfect arrow for cutting through smoke and wreckage. Upon closer inspection of the photo, I see her smile is strained from holding the pose. I had seen her more enthused heading to the store hellbent on pot roast for dinner.

Maybe my mother forgot the magnitude of my father's devotion to the magic show. As they became more settled in Alamo, she assumed he had relinquished his old dream for the charms of their new life. How wrong she was. Resurrecting the old magic show in hopes of hitting it big felt risky to her. It triggered old hurts and longings in my mother. She still harbored a secret wish to uproot the family, and she pitted her dream against his. Touring with the show versus moving us to Kingfisher, a town near Okarche, Oklahoma, where her family had settled.

One day, putting away groceries, she shoved a carton of milk in the refrigerator and said with feigned nonchalance, "Maybe we should move on back there."

It was the same old argument. Dad had just returned from work, the newspaper under his arm. With Mom's remark, his face bunched up and eyes darkened. He jabbed the air and cried, "If I move there I might as well pump gas!"

Perhaps living in Oklahoma was a hell only a great magician could understand. As I helped Mom fold up grocery bags, I exhaled, relieved Dad was so adamant. I didn't want to move there either.

"Well, Katy and I are going for a visit. I want to see my family," she said stiffly, stacking cans of beans on the shelf. To show her resolve, she had rescheduled our annual summer trip.

He scratched his head indifferently. "I got things to do here." He meant his yellow list.

⌒

Soon after, Mom and I shopped for presents to bring back to her sisters. Flipping through racks of clothes, we pulled out items with a flourish. Mom showed me a crew neck angora sweater, then shoved it back on the rack, unsure if it was Minnie Mae's style. Next came a flouncy teal blouse. "Do you think that's Ruth Ann's color?" she wondered out loud. For a long denim shirt, she made a clicking sound. She didn't know Kate's size. Mom lived with her family a long time ago. Buying presents for them was always difficult. It asked her questions she no longer knew the answers to.

We stalled by the elevators empty-handed. When Mom spied that Anne Klein burgundy suede jacket, she perked up. I followed her into the dressing room. "How do I look?" she asked, touching a cuff and turning. She looked good in everything, and her closet was packed.

Dad never said anything about the money we spent. Perhaps he didn't care or maybe he didn't know because Mom paid the bills, or he assumed Mom was practical. And she was when toilet paper was on sale. One time, she loaded an entire cart with four-packs.

Mom was the office secretary, so maybe Dad figured shopping was her paycheck. When her early American dining room set arrived with eight needlepoint cushioned chairs, he said dryly, "It's nice, honey."

Upstairs in the Junior Miss department, we found a waist-length denim jacket with fake fur. In the fitting room, I slipped it on before the mirror. Katy Gwabel peered back at me with her mouthful of flatware. My invisible crowds were rumbling through the glass. I unzipped the jacket, showing them the leopard spots inside, and felt myself give way to someone else. A bold new girl, the girl I could be in my father's magic show. I gave the mirror a sassy smile.

On the way home we sang the songs on the car radio.

Suddenly, I could hold back no longer. "I don't want to move to Oklahoma," I whined. Her face fell. "I thought you liked it there!"

Memories of the Foster clan washed over me. Their singsong chatting around a big round table, and those warm, hearty hugs from my aunts who saw me only once a year. My heart was cold.

When we returned to California from Oklahoma, she spoke no more of the virtues of moving, because she knew her appeals were hopeless. Her doubts continued to be stamped out by Dad's practiced assurances while I stood nearby, silently cheering him on as he built a case for reclaimed glory until the air felt heavy with duty and expectation.

Say yes. We can't do it without you.

A heaviness seeped into her glances and once-quick-spirited step around the house. Our life in Alamo was being diminished into something boorish and disposable. And her refrain, "I like it here," became a sappy digression.

4

CONVERSION

Lee Grabel the Magician, 1950s

EVENTUALLY MOM HAD ONLY one question left. "When?"

It was after school and we were at Lee Grabel Realty, standing around her secretary's desk. Lee Grabel was a very good magician who just wasn't very famous. Now show business was changing in his favor, and she was too good a person to renege on her claim.

When are we leaving? When will our lives change?

"Winter, 1977," he said confidently.

My heart quickened. About a year away.

"We'll need a crew of seven and a truck. Kiwanis, Lions, and Rotary will sponsor us; we'll play Oregon, Washington, Idaho; we'll be gone about four months." He stroked his chin and continued. "I got some new acts in the works, a clock routine to showcase my sleight of hand. And a flashy closer, a vanishing horse. After this tour, we'll land something big. Like Vegas."

I pulled back a little, startled. He had already decided so much. I had thought we were waiting for Mom to agree.

I suspect my mother knew from the start she didn't have a choice. Nonetheless, she didn't appear concerned as she banged out another listing on the typewriter. The rental properties would pay for the venture, and she was grateful for that.

"Let's get this show on the road!" he called out. His row of disorderly teeth dazzled me. I felt lightheaded.

Suddenly, my parents looked at me. Something moved across their faces, perhaps a sliver of doubt as to whether taking their young daughter along would be prudent. My eyelids fell.

"Katy can jump out of the top hat," Dad said, and I made a sound of relief.

Jumping out of that top hat must be an important job. I imagined breaching its golden rim, the dressed-up little darling of a grand bedazzled spectacle. It wasn't the same as singing my hit songs at the Hollywood Bowl, but within the magic show's realm of light, I would no longer be Katy Gwabel, that shy, slouching girl.

I met my father's steady, blue-eyed gaze. At that moment, our relationship changed. To him I wasn't a kid anymore or a straight man to his jokes. I was a caretaker of his magic show and bound to a solemn agreement I didn't understand. And to me, he wasn't my overworked father anymore. He had shed that crusty old skin and now he was my dream maker, the giver of wishes, the one who would put me on a fancy stage in the spotlight.

Now that it was official, he spun around with the verve of a circus ringmaster. "Here we come, world!" We laughed like indulged children.

That night I sang a cappella to my invisible crowds. Perched on the edge of my bed, I crooned an Elton John ballad with all the heartfelt sadness I could muster. No gallivanting around with my pink hairbrush microphone, no blaring record player and imagined fanfare—just my voice. It satisfied me in a way my frantic rock star pretending didn't.

Even with all my earnest effort, I could not ignore my awful singing. My voice wasn't very pretty. It was feeble, a tremor on the tongue, something breakable. I appeared to be straining against unseen forces. Setting aside the album, I lay down on my bed, saddened by how unbeautiful my voice was.

I could always learn to sing. In fact, there were all kinds of classes and groups for girls who wanted to sing and dance. Yet the memory of those mocking sixth-grade girls always dissuaded me. I dreaded failing, being criticized and laughed at. I hadn't told Mom about those classes because she would insist I go. She said I spent too much time in my room. I closed my eyes, hoping to block out the clamor of my big, unreachable dreams. Sometimes it was too much, all that squelched fire.

The magic show would be easy. I'd get to dress up, jump out of that big hat, and hand Dad things onstage. No one would laugh at or judge me, and I wouldn't have to learn something I was bad at. I could be onstage without any risk. In old show photos, the assistants stood in the background holding props. I'd be good at that.

On my desk I had a binder filled with stories I'd written in neat pencil. Stories about flying girls, lonely girls, and girls who governed the galaxy from their bedrooms, stories I never showed anyone. Somehow my place in the magic show felt right. Maybe I'd always remain, as I knew myself to be, a girl with a story untold.

II

INNER SANCTUM OF MAGIC

To excel in anything, you have to be a little neurotic.

—LEE GRABEL

5

ce

NO SUCH THING AS MAGIC

Return to the road, 1977

THE MAGIC BEGAN WITH power tools.

Upstairs in my bedroom, I heard sawing, drilling, and hammering from the garage. Dad had cleared out a space to build a masterful new illusion for the finale called The Vanishing Horse. Sometimes I heard the garage door shutting and his brisk steps through the house and then out the front door. He would return from the hardware store with bags of metal gizmos. More sawing, drilling, and hammering. Once, when he wasn't there, I peeked inside the garage. An angular shape draped in a tarp filled the space. It was big. Very big. What was it?

I kept finding myself an outsider to all these immense happenings. I wanted to help him mobilize the magic show, whereas he wanted nothing from me at all. Each morning, he reached into his jacket pocket and removed his yellow list, and I'd see those mysterious scribbles that would somehow breathe life into our stranded show.

One afternoon Mom told me to bring her the frozen hamburger

from the freezer in the garage. When I opened the door, I saw that mysterious shape undraped. It was a large open platform with no sides, tall enough to stand in. At each corner, decorative curved wooden beams connected the top and bottom portions.

The contraption was midnight blue with wide black trim, heavy and sturdy, as if birthed whole from a large primordial tree. Dad stood inside with his head up, studying its dark interior surface with a power saw in his work glove. His work clothes consisted of a banana-yellow tennis cap with air holes and old plaid golf pants splattered with paint.

This peculiar apparatus had been absent from the old show photos. Later, I found out its name was the Flora Dora, and it had belonged to my parents' old friend Dante the Magician, who passed it on to my father. Dad flipped on the saw, and a deafening roar filled my ears as he cut into the wood above his head. Sawdust sprayed away from the blade and settled in little tributaries below his feet. A rectangular piece of wood fell away. I realized the top portion was much larger than it appeared due to the deceptive black border. Actually, the entire top was hollow.

I learned later that the hollow area is known in stage conjuring as a *trap*. The trap is the secret heart of magic, a compartment small enough to blend into the average proportions of a piece of equipment yet large enough to fit a woman lying flat as a rug or curled up as tight as a napping feline. My father was simply enlarging the opening of the trap. When he was finished and turned off the saw, he carefully inspected the trap's width and height, its clean edges, and the promise of its shadowy interior.

Dad moved fast around the house and slow in the garage. That's how he built. He thought deeply and then picked up a tool. He was very comfortable in his workshop, as he had built much of his show. His work was less fine carpentry than functional and strong, and he knew how to use trim to make equipment appear smaller than it was. As a builder, he didn't have to buy stock illusions and therefore could add original touches.

Not wanting to disturb his focus, I moved silently toward the freezer and opened the door.

"Kate, tell your mother to come in," I heard him say behind me.

When I returned with my mother, he pointed to the floor of the Flora Dora and said casually, "Lie down, honey."

He was constructing another trap in the bottom half. She kicked off her high heels, and, in her best gabardine slacks, lowered herself limb by limb. She curled up so tight her knees kissed her forehead.

Sensing the reverent secrecy in this, I pushed back my shoulders, suddenly conscious of my bad posture. I had finally entered the inner sanctum of the magic show.

Dad drew the outline of Mom's form on the wood with white chalk. Then she gracefully unwound herself and stood up, patting her hair in place, as if to say, *Ho-hum, this again.* Mom: 26 by 32 by 15. He had been constructing illusions around her measurements in a fetal curl for a very long time.

On her way out she announced, "I got rhubarb pie for tonight."

I followed her, then turned around. Dad was bent down on one knobby knee, studying those chalk lines. I thought he was going to mark it again, like Einstein seized by divine inspiration at a chalkboard. I wanted to slip over to the bench, sit down and watch. Something important was happening here. Chalk lines were drawn; serrated blades cut through wood while a trillion metal gizmos were torqued and pounded. Somehow vanishing a horse required all these little tasks, a secret recipe.

Dad started walking around the Flora Dora, examining the white marks from all angles. Silence. I had hoped the magic show would bring my father and me together. Instead, I had not budged much from where I was before—static and shadow.

⁓

A few days later, when I returned home from school, a very big crate sat in the backyard by our aquamarine, kidney-shaped pool. Dad unlatched the lid. Inside was a figure swaddled in plastic. He ripped away the sides of the box with a crowbar and unwrapped layer upon layer of packing plastic, circling around, pulling it aside until a shape appeared. An animal with four legs. He cut away the last strip of packing, and there it was—a horse. Or rather a swaybacked old sorrel mare that had been stuffed and mounted by a taxidermist.

"Poor thing," Mom said woefully. "We'll have to find an ugly one just to match her."

It never occurred to me The Vanishing Horse would have two horses, one real and one fake.

"They won't see it for long," Dad assured us.

A stitch of doubt creased Mom's face. "I certainly hope not."

I understood then that the audience must think this was a real horse. Maybe they'd be fooled except it didn't move, not a leg or wither or flank.

"You'll have to do this onstage"—Dad walked over to the horse's rear and gave us a wide-eyed goofy face while he slyly reached over and swished its tail—"so that they'll think it's real." Even though he poked fun at himself, he really expected the audience to be tricked this way.

Mom smiled at his schoolboy's folly. "Sure, Lee."

He petted its back. "It's our closing number."

I walked around it, running my fingers along the short umber hair.

Mom tilted her head at the horse and frowned. "I guess I'll be getting a bill from a taxidermist."

Mom had been sitting at her walnut dropleaf desk, writing checks to the local hardware store, and now this.

"And a bill for a truck." He firmly nodded his head. "We must have one." The Broadway Magical Mystery Extravaganza was a road show, after all.

Mom flicked away the horse's forelock from its glass eyes and sighed. "Don't you want to see the mess you're in?"

Suddenly, Dad turned to me, his eyes flaming. "Don't go telling your friends about this horse here," he ordered. My excitement plunged. He had me pinned as some blabbermouth kid. Then I remembered the incident in the fourth grade. I had asked him to teach me his best card trick for Show and Tell. Then, during class, after I'd performed the trick for my classmates, I'd revealed how it was done. He never forgot it.

"I won't, I won't," I told him, as ever, regretting my loose regard of the cardinal rule of professional magic. I would never tell the secrets of my father's magic ever again. I really believed that then.

As we moved into spring, Dad started scribbling on his big tablet of yellow paper after dinner. He called it "formulating." I saw rune shapes, exaggerated arrows, three-dimensional boxes, and numbers with dollar signs. Formulating did not require a list; it was like dreaming on paper.

One day he came home with foam rubber, gray duct tape, and aluminum sheet metal. It was for his new routine called The Clocks, far different from the usual magician fare.

"It's going to be an original number," he said, reaching into his pants pockets. I heard the jingle of keys and hardware. He removed a few small screws. In his flat open palm, they were glimmering excavated gems. "I don't want anyone thinking I'm just a box pusher," he declared.

As the weeks passed, preparation for the tour continued. Dad wanted a smile befitting his exalted return to the stage, so his crooked teeth were fitted with sterling braces. He also bought a white truck with a forty-foot trailer and hired a Mr. Bly to book shows across the western states. Mr Bly would call Dad with updates: Ukiah, Coos Bay, Bellingham, Pocatello... Dad always ended the conversations with, "Send the paperwork, and Helene will type it up!"

One night in April, Mom stood at the kitchen counter, shuffling through the mail. She breathed a sigh of relief that there were no surprises that day. Just dental bills. She pulled the pot roast from the oven and jabbed a fork into a red potato. "Tell your father."

In the garage, a hailstorm of nails, bolts, and screws had left his work area in disarray. He sat on his workbench in his tennis cap with legs crossed, reminding me of a man accustomed to sitting. I skidded to a halt. Something was wrong.

Slowly poking around his tool kit, he squinted at a metal doodad and said, "Hell if I can find the right bit." He then knocked the lid closed and gestured toward the dirty window. "It would have been beautiful on the seventeenth hole today."

His hustle and bustle was gone. I'd never seen him so unconsumed by the magic show, so depleted of the fire that had been propelling him for weeks.

"Dinner's ready," I said lightly, hoping my words would jar him out of this strange malaise.

The Flora Dora, with its menacing gaps, innards, and fissures, loomed down on him. He'd been demoted from its supreme master into a suburban flunky with an unmanageable crafts project. A small propane heater did a pitiful job of heating the garage at night, and Dad's thin nose had brightened to crimson. His work gloves lay on the ground with fingers splayed, holding air, and his hair was as thin and white as paper.

Worried, I rubbed my knuckle along my metal teeth. Had he lost faith in the enterprise? *Please not that*, I thought. We both needed the magic show to free ourselves from our frivolous drama before our mirrors and to finally materialize the crowds for which we yearned. Hugging my forearms, I braced myself for the worst.

"Here I am, your ol' dad," he said sorrowfully, "acting like I have good sense." His hooded eyes met mine. Hearing him talk this way was too distressing. I lowered my eyes.

Maybe he was finally grasping the challenges before him. Revamping the magic show would be costly, and he didn't know if ticket sales would recoup his investment. Although my mother was willing to cooperate, she didn't understand his hunger for glory at their age; if he wanted to play the big leagues, he would have to compete with young, brazen magicians with fancy hydraulic equipment and heads of thick, raven hair. In that lucid moment, he had glimpsed the improbability of his big dream.

I didn't know then what I know now. My father could never have stopped this venture, even if he'd wanted to. No one chooses to be a magician. It chooses whom it chooses.

In the garage he slowly stood up, hands on his knees. "Come on, your mother is waiting." I followed his slow, lumbering gait into the kitchen.

Nonetheless, the next morning, the hammering, sawing, and drilling resumed. Mr. Bly's package arrived filled with contracts from Kiwanis, Lions, and Rotary clubs. Dad signed his name, binding us to a contractual obligation to bring magic to strangers across five states.

Over the next few days, I thought about Dad's moment of uncertainty. One night my imagination percolated, and—*pop, pop!*—an idea seized me. I sat down and penned a story about a traveling magician. Before each show, the magician would sit in his dressing room and decide he was lonely, tired of the road, and wanted to work at his brother's dry-cleaning shop. But once his show started and the crowd applauded, he realized how much he loved his show. And then when the crowd left and the stage darkened, he would sit in his dressing room and decide he was lonely, tired of the road, and wanted to work in his brother's dry-cleaning shop. That's how the story ended. The magician forever vacillating between wanting to flee his show and loving it. I read my eleven pages out loud, noting how my words lived, breathed, and commanded space. I was fired up and ready to write more.

"I'm writing stories," I announced to Mom in the kitchen that night.

Dad, walking in the door with another bag of metal gadgets, heard this and advised, "Nothing happens unless you make it happen."

This was his oft-said motto of self-responsibility.

I told Mom I needed more binder paper, and the next day she returned from the store with several packages, including a little purple notebook. Upstairs in my bedroom, I inspected it. It was a reporter's pad, what journalists use for a news story. I admired its compact shape. A handy size, small enough to fit in my purse. I wrote down Dad's elevator joke and maxim, *nothing happens unless you make it happen.* I flipped it closed and flipped it open, studying the thin blue lines, neat margins, and blank pages. A mysterious passion for that little book overcame me.

Within those empty white pages was a veiled invitation. It was the first time I recorded anything about my father, the first time it occurred to me he was interesting enough to do so. I didn't understand the excitement I felt in seeing my few written words. Such an innocuous thing, that little purple notebook. Still, my father and I would eventually launch a covert battle over ownership of those blank white pages.

⌐

The core issue was publicity. The magic show needed something big. In the old days, local newspapers covered the show. Except for a bit of film footage, those articles were, and still are, the only recording of his big illusion show in the fifties. None of his attempts to land national exposure had worked back then. He used to send press releases filled with old-fashioned hyperbole to the *Saturday Evening Post,* a popular national magazine of the day. I once found a brochure with a photo of him in a fedora sitting on a white fence before a pasture. The caption read: "Grabel in his California ranch and workshop in the 1950s." Ranch? When I asked my mother, she laughed and called it "publicity." Some of his press releases also claimed that my mother had turned down a lead role with movie star John Wayne to work in the show.

His failure to entice the *Post* into covering his show taught him that legitimate journalism was sensitive to anything that could be perceived as disguised advertising. A floating piano was not necessarily newsworthy.

For our upcoming tour he added *Reader's Digest* to his yellow list. This weekly national periodical was full of human-interest stories, some written by average people about their unusual experiences. Stories were commonly about heroic deeds, dogs, preachers, mothers, farm life…many of them inspirational and heartwarming.

As the tour neared, I suspect he spent many summer evenings on the patio amid Mom's potted geraniums, considering different journalistic angles, hooks, or slants that could secure the show a place on *Reader's Digest*'s modest yet far-reaching pages. He could not write it himself. It would have oozed with blatant self-promotion.

Unless he could find another way.

I imagine his hand tapping his list as he formulated his plan each night. *Tap tap tap—Reader's Digest—tap tap tap—publicity—tap tap tap.* Then one night he got it. He wrote my name and underlined it.

The next day, from the foot of the stairs, Dad called to me, "Come on! Let's get this show on the road!" and we jumped into the Cadillac.

I tagged along to the fabric store, hardware depot, sheet metal shop, and lumberyard. He needed shims, wedges, two-by-fours, wire, a ruler, varnish, alphabet address labels, and soldering tools. It appeared the magic show was an odd amalgam of everyday objects arranged on a tabletop altar. I felt short-circuited from my body, intoxicated by the excitement of it all as we drove through the spring foliage, bobbing in and out of stores, crossing items off his list.

Once, when the car got quiet, he tapped his head and smiled. "I'm formulating," he said. He also confided to me the truth about professional magic. "It's all hokum, Kate," he said. "Some do hokum. We do *sophisticated* hokum." Later he sternly advised, "You get a job with security." He wanted me to have an easier life than he did. "You be a teacher, bank teller, or escrow girl." Then we cruised the local horse stables in search of a vanishing horse and found one. A pretty chestnut Shetland Arabian mare, unbroken and gentle, that regarded us through a hank of hair with two deep, wondrous eyes.

The next day I sat on the paint-flecked bench in the garage, an official inductee into the inner sanctum of the show. I held a big glass of a newfangled drink that Mom had whipped up in the blender. A banana, orange, and pineapple juice concoction that was easy on the teeth, as both our dentists had tightened our braces that day. I sipped the drink and watched Dad affix a black metal arm from inside the top trap to the horse's head, between its two ears. The long slender metal bar, with its pointy elbow joint, would help assistants maneuver the stuffed horse into the trap for its vanishing stunt. Dad tightened the screws with quick twists of his wrist.

"I got an idea," he said in a silky voice. "Why don't you write an article about the tour for *Reader's Digest*?"

I blinked. The remark, though phrased as a question, was clearly said as a statement, a task to be completed. *Why don't you write an article about the tour for* Reader's Digest? Didn't I want to help Dad resurrect the magic show? Yes, I did.

"It could be a cute story," he continued, waving his screwdriver with the flair of a conductor. "A daughter of a magician, traveling in her father's show. Unusual enough." He had found an angle for his article—*my* story of the road.

It wasn't such a farfetched idea. I'd written that story about the magician. Journalism was different, yet still writing. I loved the industrious feeling of sitting at my bedroom desk, penning letters to friends. I also read all kinds of books. Sometimes I cracked them open and inhaled them with the delight of a mad librarian. Still, I thought those *Reader's Digest* magazines dull and old hat. I had seen them only in the waiting rooms of dentists and pediatricians.

"It would give the show a real boost," he said with the authority of a marketing whiz. "Just the kind of national exposure we need to impress those casinos." He stuck a pink feather tiara of tinsel on the horse's forelock. That tiara had become an essential prop for the routine as he needed it to conceal the metal bar sticking up. It was hard for me to imagine folks not being suspicious of a stationary horse with a funny hat. I feared we were veering into the lowlands of hokum.

He joined me on the bench and we both sipped our drinks, wiping the mustaches from our upper lips. "You know," he said, swirling the foamy liquid, "television opportunities might come our way."

Later, I would wonder if he'd actually said *The Tonight Show Starring Johnny Carson* or if our two minds, linked together, had silently injected each other with that notion.

"You want to be a writer, don't you?" My color rose. I wished he hadn't heard me declare my writing intentions to Mom a few days before. Those empty white pages in my little purple notebook didn't feel the same anymore, not with this new request. Something was being claimed of me, and I didn't know what. Any hesitation was blotted out by the promises of the magic show. If writing a *Reader's Digest* story about our tour would interest a casino or win a spot on *The Tonight Show*, then I would do it. For that I would do anything. Also—I wanted to please him.

On the day I was born, my father had composed one of his yellow lists. He'd dropped my mother off at the hospital, showed a few houses, picked up a building permit at the county offices, and called prospective clients. At the bottom of the list was probably this: Stop by the hospital. Deep inside, I knew I wasn't high up on his list.

"I'll do it," I said with genuine enthusiasm. We both smiled, our braces matching silver grids of dirty light.

6

A FEW HELPERS

Lee and Helen with Cindy, 1950s

I ASSUMED MY PARENTS' former show crew would travel with us again. Dad dismissed that notion. "They have families and jobs," he told me. "They can't just leave."

We were sitting at our favorite restaurant next to big slanted windows that overlooked San Francisco Bay, dotted with rippling white sails.

"We need Al," Mom told him, bringing an amber Manhattan to her lips. The Great Alexander had been their truck driver and lead assistant for years.

With a decisive hand gesture he shot that down. "We'll have to find new people." Al had a job managing a trailer park, and Dad refused to ask him to leave for a few months' work.

We needed three male stage assistants, two to load and unload the truck, and another to drive the truck and set up the piano each night. And one female stage assistant who would also be my tutor. Their absence occupied a palpable space in the tour's planning.

"How will we find them?" I asked.

"I'll just produce them." He snapped his fingers. "Alakazam!"

We exchanged smiles of steel and wire while Mom lifted her eyebrows in surprise and fished a dripping maraschino cherry from the golden liquid. "You ran out of answers on that one, huh?" she remarked, popping the cherry in her mouth.

In the old days, they usually hired young men who came backstage looking for work—bright-eyed roamers, able-bodied idealists, the gifted and the misunderstood, those un-soothed by the sameness of days. Men who were enchanted by the scrappy magic show's pleasures, trances, and wizardry. Many tours could pass, lulled by the rhythm of the road. Seventeen years later, that pool of reliable workers was lost to my parents. The times had changed, and they didn't know where to look.

In the summer of 1976, seven months before our tour, my parents placed an ad in the *Oakland Tribune*. "Wanted: Assistants in a Traveling Magic Show."

It would certainly draw interest, perhaps the wrong kind—prima donnas or those with serious theatrical aspirations who would resent the heave-ho the job demanded. Defining what qualities my parents wanted was not easy, something so intrinsic, so natural to a magic show, it was hard to name: hardy souls, easygoing, kindred spirits, resolute and committed, sharing affinities and blood oaths, something tribal.

Since we needed a female assistant, I hoped Cindy would step in. She was twenty-three years old and worked in an office, typing and answering phones. She sewed her own dresses and rescued kitties from the pound. As a teenager, she had ruled the house with her loud hippie music and the heavy tread of her boots up and down the stairs. She wore a suede jacket with fringe swinging from the sleeves. When she turned eighteen and moved out, Dad had the same remark for Cindy. *Whatdoyouknowyou'rejustalittlegirl.*

No trace of the plodding teenager remained. She had matured into a soft-spoken, thoughtful young woman, quiet and prone to fierce opinions. Mom and I would meet her for lunch, where she ordered plain white fish and sipped chamomile tea with the decorum of a princess. She wanted to marry and start a family, yet none of the men she dated, as much as they adored her, was the right one.

One night she arrived for dinner and stood in the doorway with her sun-streaked brown hair falling around her tan shoulders. She wore a silk skirt that swayed around her knees. Her clothes never clung to her ribs or behind. Everything flowed as softly, naturally, as her cascading hair. Her sheer silk skirts and gypsy blouses with long, puffy sleeves were always in motion, rippling and streaming as if she were constantly caught in a breeze.

"Hello, Katy, how are you?" she asked gently. Each time I saw her, she would ask with keen interest, *how are you?* Apparently, she really wanted to know. I rebuffed her whenever I could. When she lived with us, she treated me as an annoying urchin, and I was going to make her pay.

"Fine," I answered stiffly.

As my parents' agreeable dining and shopping companion, I smugly saw myself as their favorite. Also, I was jealous she had traveled in the magic show as a young girl. I had heard plenty of endearing stories about Cindy growing up on the road. In one town, Mom took her trick-or-treating in a taxi with a hotel sheet thrown over her head.

Sometimes, I ushered Cindy around the house, showing her Mom's new furniture and my album collection in my bedroom. On this particular night, I led her to Dad's little office next to the stairs and updated her on the progress of the show—the Flora Dora, the new truck, the stuffed horse, the towns that were booked, Sacramento, Bakersfield, Lancaster…She sweetly smiled and touched my arm. "How exciting this is for you!" I felt a stab of disappointment. No spark of envy in her calm, watchful eyes. Nothing.

I pointed to one of Dad's old lithographs on the wall that Mom had recently framed. We both gazed at it. His sharply sculpted face blazed down on us, a minister at a pulpit delivering a fervent sermon to his flock. We were silent. Some fathers were accountants, dentists, or plumbers.

Cindy pushed back a golden lock of long hair. I noted her fingers were so slender she had to wrap her rings with string to prevent them from falling off. She felt so soft, safe, and still, so unknown to me, an angel, a floater, a visitor of happenstance who by birth found herself in the wrong realm of magic. My posturing was a way of concealing how much I missed her around the house. I hoped trouping together would give us the sister time we hadn't had because of our age difference. Maybe we would share sweaters and bags of popcorn on the road. I wanted to absorb her with my senses, wear her clothes, sleep on her pillow, and use her shampoo.

Please come with us.

That's when I laid the big whopper on her. I told her the tour might be just the beginning. "Television opportunities might come our way," I gloated.

Clasping her hands together, she again exclaimed, "How exciting all this is for you!" An ache seized my throat. She was only being polite.

Cindy didn't want to join us. She had her own dream to become a wife and mom, to take her kids on camping trips, picnics, and museum outings, fix them pancakes on Saturdays and pizzas on Tuesdays. The kind of childhood she didn't get growing up on the road. While we traveled with the show, she would be sitting at her secretary's desk, compiling a list of baby names. I was dismayed that this, of all things, would bring her happiness. My sister aspired for the ordinary. Later on, when we were hurtling down the road, I would sit in the back of our car and think of my poor sister at home, with her small, unfabulous dreams.

⌢

Time moved on. Summer turned into fall. My fourteenth birthday passed, and I started counting the days till our first show, on February 7th. One day Mr. Bly called with a listing of more towns: Walla Walla, Tacoma, Yakima, Spokane...

"You'll have to tell your parents," Mom remarked to Dad.

He nodded his head, only appeasing her. When Grandma and Grandpa Grabeel visited us from Portland, he covered the Flora Dora with a tarp and instructed me not to speak of the upcoming tour.

"I'll tell them later," he said.

My grandfather never understood Dad's attraction to the magic show, and he was relieved when he finally quit for what grandfather considered to be *real employment*. My father knew his return to magic would distress his father.

Meanwhile, Dad started soldering sheets of shiny thin aluminum into round-bodied clocks for his new routine. As for finding our new crew, we had made no progress.

"Why don't you ask the Magic Gals?" Mom suggested one day.

The Magic Gals was the name of a club for wives of magicians. Mom hosted parties for them, and the wives always brought their husbands along. Dad grimaced. He suffered through those parties. Some of the guests were his old friends who once had popular acts in the theater circuit, while others were dabblers in magic. It was the latter group he endured. It hurt his pride to fraternize with hobby magicians.

One day in October, Mom slid a roast in the oven for the Magic Gal party that afternoon and told Dad, "Be nice. We need their help."

Suddenly, his face flared red and he implored, "Why did you invite them?" He meant those irritating lowbrow hobbyists. "I don't have anything in common with them!"

"Lee! For goodness' sake! Of course you do," she protested.

He stormed around the kitchen, flailing his arms, and indignantly declared, "It's below me. To associate. With amateurs!"

The hierarchy of professional magic was meaningless to Mom when she had guests to feed. She screwed up her face and gasped, "What are you talking about?"

I stood to the side, head turning from parent to parent.

"Claude!" he yelped. "He's never even done a show. He sits at home and pretends!"

Sweet Claude. He brought me little magic tricks and had the face of a cherub.

"And Radcliff Jones. He can't even do sleight of hand." Dad furiously gestured into the air. "He does little gimmick tricks!"

I shuddered. Once I saw Radcliff Jones insert his teeth into his mouth before dinner.

Mom leaned over the sink, frantically pulling away husks from cobs of corn, trying to stay calm. "Lee, what am I supposed to do? They're going to be here soon."

"After what we've done with the Big Show, I shouldn't even be talking to these people!" he charged, his mouth in a hard line.

"They might know somebody," she countered.

"They won't *know anyone*," he muttered and marched off.

Mom called after him, "Bring in extra chairs!"

He reluctantly carried them in and then followed Mom's directives from the kitchen, to wash off the patio and arrange the outdoor furniture. As I set up the buffet table with napkins and hot plates, I watched him mope around outside, a victim of an unjust crime.

At party time, the wives trotted in the door in colorful muumuus and dangling earrings, heavily perfumed, bearing casseroles and jabbering loudly. Behind them in a fussy hubbub trudged the magicians, knotted and stooped, pink cheeks newly shaved, their V-neck shirts revealing thin patches of chest hair.

Right away they got down to business. With old card decks and trick gimmicks stuffed in their trouser pockets, they headed for the ice bucket to talk shop.

"You deal a second this way."

"The little pinkie here."

"Use a long card, see?"

"If you're gonna throw cards, they gotta be nylon."

Or sometimes they did not talk at all. Pulling out a deck or laying a coin in the center of a palm silently invited an exchange of tricks. It went back and forth—a break, a crimp, a pass, a foam ball slipped between hands, or a handkerchief tip poking out of a fist. They were simple pocket effects or routine gimmicks picked up at a magic depot. Showing their tricks to another magician was like finding a citizen of their own country. Meanwhile, the women chatted among themselves and completely ignored them.

I passed them crackers.

"Your mom got more of those little onions?" one of them asked me, holding up a martini stem glass.

My parents had met them at the Oakland chapter of the Magic Circle. They were much older than my parents, a hodgepodge of theatrical talent from the last days of vaudeville and big band floor acts. The men wore dapper polyester suits with thin gold chains around their necks and smelled of stale aftershave. Guests included Mr. Friday Night, known for a popular drunk magic act; Mazzie, a magician and former member of a vaudevillian juggling duo; The Amazing Zogie, who gave up his cushy job with the US Postal Service after a flattering review in *Variety*; and Wally, a former burlesque magician whose dirty jokes used to knock them dead at private stag parties.

I went to the kitchen to help Mom. "Go out to the freezer and get me the frozen peas," she said.

Dad leaned in close and said softly, "Lock the door behind you."

I passed the smoke-filled room of gravelly voices and slipped inside the garage. Dad had covered the stuffed horse and Flora Dora for the party. Suspicions ran high. Maybe he feared these magicians were on the Magic Castle payroll and, just when he was carving into the roast beef, they would sneak into his garage and whip out their James Bond cameras.

During the party, the hobby magicians were excited about Dad's return to the stage.

"We'll finally get to see that floating piano of yours!" they said with genuine delight.

The pros, on the other hand, were dismayed. They'd given their lives to their acts, which left them broke and scrambling for new employment when entertainment switched to television. They surrounded Dad with their warnings and aspersions.

"The road's dead."

"You gone flaky?"

"End up in the poor house."

"You got a good thing here."

Dad gazed over their heads as if they were too short to see the parade. He figured himself sharper than these guys. "What about another drink, fellas?"

Afterward, Mazzie shuffled up to Dad, rubbing his jacket lapel between his stubby fingers. "You got a crew for that show of yours?" he asked.

Dad grunted.

"I got a nephew looking for work. Brody, good kid," he said warmly. "Show him a magic trick. It'll be good for him."

7

THE LEE GRABEL FAN CLUB

Lee and young Katy

DAD HIRED BRODY, WHO told us that his cousin, Ben, also
needed work. Ben was hired, and the two boys joined the show as
our stage assistants and packing muscle. Dad named Ben the official
animal caretaker in charge of three geese, six doves, and our young
mare, Frankie. From the newspaper ad, Dad also found two more
crew members. Clair, a recent college graduate with a teacher's certifi-
cate, was our box jumper and my tutor. Our truck driver, Rick, was a
friendly man who used to haul tomatoes.

On a November night, our new crew sat around the dining room
table licking their fingers over Mom's fried chicken as a big, festive din
filled the house. In more than two months, we would be gone.

Rick considered himself an expert in everything, especially floating
pianos. When Dad told him the piano needed repairs, he rocked his
big body on his cowboy boots and touched his pointy chin. "A little
oil on the joints will get it rising," he figured.

Across the table from me sat the cousins, Mazzie's nephews,

Brody and Ben, frisky boys in white sneakers and baseball caps with a bounce in their walk. They reminded me of jocks without teams, eager for someone to throw them a ball. They called me "Brace Face" or "Metal Mouth" or they messed up the top of my head into a shaggy-dog hairdo.

Roughhousing was their pastime, and they did it often, punching each other in the stomach or falling into a mock wrestler's frozen embrace. After a meal they often accused each other of farting. They constantly exchanged wisecracks and punch lines to jokes they found particularly hilarious. Most of the time no one understood what was so funny. I watched them tilt their beer bottles with abandon before going for seconds.

Ben was a tall twenty-two-year-old with sandy bangs that edged his soft brown eyes. He was very polite and accompanied his requests—"Pass the butter, thank you" or "Another beer, please"—with a big, sunny smile, revealing perfect white teeth. On top of his head, three cowlicks pointed in three different directions, giving the impression he was continuously waking up from a nap. Brody, his muddy brown hair infused with a little fruity red, was shorter than his cousin. Under his cap, his locks gathered in loose, dancing curls. He was nineteen years old, just out of high school, and not as easy around folks as his older cousin.

The only crew member who really intrigued me was Clair, a neat, tidy girl with a gentle demeanor. Clair drank beer with the boys and then dabbed a napkin on the corners of her mouth. Her simple no-fuss haircut revealed her curlicue ears. Around her neck she wore an alphabet necklace, all the letters fused together, *ABCDE*, into a conga line. She easily fell into the sway of the cousins' comedic banter, grasped the humor that I didn't understand, and had a certain credibility when she rolled her eyes and said, "You *guys*."

I suspect Clair and the cousins felt rather charmed to be there. Their search for normal employment had landed them in a traveling illusion show. Around the table the pending adventure felt alive with promise. All of us were ceaselessly smiling at each other over our chicken legs and pulley bones. As Clair and the cousins chatted comfortably, I scrambled for a way to be included and decided on Dad's hallmark joke. When I delivered the final, "No steps!" I was horrified by their impassive faces regarding me across the table.

Clair set down her fork. "Maybe you could show me your math book," she said in a teacherly way. "I need to know what you're working on."

"Okay," I weakly responded. Inside, I was stunned. Clair actually considered me her student!

Palling around with my parents had distorted my sense of social position with adults, and I didn't perceive myself as a kid. I assumed the crew would be my friends. When the tour started, I learned otherwise. Our age differences inevitably kept us apart.

At the end of the meal, Ben requested hot chocolate. "Could I have marshmallows, please?" He was quite endearing with his unflinching grin. Mom found an old bag from God knows which long-ago birthday party. Brody dumped sugar in his coffee and Clair sipped herbal tea. Mom topped the pecan pie with dollops of whipped cream.

At the foot of the table, Dad's head tilted back as inspiration seized him. "Here, let me show you something," he announced, making good on Mazzie's request. He stood up and gestured that he wanted a cigarette from the pack in Rick's pocket. Rick handed him one and Dad lit it, taking a quick drag. A puff of smoke drifted out from his rounded lips. Then he did it again. Opening his mouth for all to see, he picked up the burning cigarette with his tongue. I held my breath. It perched on the tip, a surfer on a wave, in perfect balance. Then he drew in his tongue and closed his mouth around it. From his lips he blew another waft of smoke, as if he had conceived smoke from a flame deep within. He continued dancing the cigarette around his tongue, closing his mouth on it and blowing smoke. The air smoldered. No one said a word.

I felt ash and heat in my mouth, smoke in my throat. I wanted to gag and laugh at the same time. I glanced at Brody across the table. His face was red, contorted and smiling. Watching my father eat a cigarette evoked delight and pain. Brody had felt it, too. I studied the smattering of acne on his jaw, that familiar slouch I'd seen in myself.

Then Brody's voice broke the silence. He sounded slightly dazed when he asked, "How'd you do that?"

Dad snuffed out the cigarette in a saucer and shrugged. "I burnt my tongue so many times, I got nicotine poisoning," he told us plainly.

I felt a tinge of disappointment. I wanted him to speak of angel transmissions at dawn or cigars dancing the Watusi. I knew better. Magic didn't *just happen*. Vanishing a horse required many trips to the hardware store.

Across the table, Dad's story of toil didn't lessen the awe on Brody's face. All his joshing and jesting had ceased as he turned two guileless gray eyes in Dad's direction. His body was straight and alert even as his whiskey-brown curls appeared tousled by imaginary weather. I smiled at him, cautiously. It was possible Brody needed our magic show as much as I did. To impress others, for attention, for the praise of strangers. Brody and I watched Dad eat Mom's pie, scraping up the last crumbs with the melting vanilla ice cream dripping from his fork.

Whatever glories we hoped the magic show would give us, Lee Grabel was our man.

_ɔ_

The next day, when the boys and Rick showed up, the garage doors opened and the dark-green crates started rolling down the driveway to the white truck parked below. The show was being moved to a warehouse at the Alameda County Fairgrounds for rehearsal. I stood in the doorway watching, feeling the house become less lopsided as each box left the garage, strands of cobwebs falling away. The magic show was finally free.

As the crew maneuvered the crates downhill, they nearly slipped from their clutches, as if eager for the open road. The daylight exposed their poor condition. The crates were battered, nicked, and cracked, with tarnished hasps, and corners worn down to raw splinters. A few were so dilapidated, they swayed on their joints.

The liberated show energized Dad. Occasionally, he clapped his hands together and called out, "Come on, kids!" and led them to the next crate. Brody followed behind him, outpacing Ben's slow lope and panting Rick.

"What about this one?" Brody would ask Dad, or, "Which one's next?"

Dad bathed them with a medley of slapstick gags as they charged around. Pointing, he said, "Watch out!" and when Brody turned his head, he tagged his stomach. That ol' misdirection. Soon, everyone was laughing and sweating. He told Ben, our animal caretaker, with fake sincerity, "Didn't I tell you about the lion production?"

When I brought them glasses of water, they were standing in our empty garage, smiling.

"I have a good feeling about this show, Mr. Grabel!" Rick exclaimed.

Mom and I walked around the garage with hands on our hips and exclaimed, "Get a load of this!" Our voices bounced off the walls and unfilled space. Our sensible, straight house didn't feel right. Now that the show was loose in the world, I could already feel its demands.

The guys gathered up their jackets. They now had to unload the truck at the fairgrounds. "Hold on, fellas," Dad said. He dashed into the house and returned with a coffee cup. I heard tinkling inside and knew it was packed with ice and his favorite single malt scotch.

"Let's go," he yipped and tossed his car keys to Brody. "You drive!" Then he added with an exaggerated wink, "I'll tell you my secrets." Brody smoothly slipped inside the leather seats of the Cadillac and adjusted the mirror.

Ben joined Rick in the truck. Our driveway was steep and curved, and Dad gave Brody instructions when he was backing down. Right away Brody hit our green hedge that bordered the driveway. He halted the car and started again, twisting the wheel, jerking forward and back, all the way down the hill while Dad frantically tried to keep his glass upright. At the bottom of the hill, they sped off with a little bush limb caught in the fender.

8

BOX JUMPERS AND ROADIES

The Broadway Magical Mystery Extravaganza

THE BIG TOP HAT was glossy gold, with a sports car's buffed shine, and appeared to rumble from its own souped-up motor. I saw it my first day at the warehouse, a circus cast-off on a low pedestal amid battered crates. I peered inside. It was shaped with ribbed wire and lined with thin black felt, large enough to fit a young woman hugging her knees. The scent of perfume and tobacco rose from its center as if it was the closet of an unchaste showgirl.

On the other side of the warehouse sat the celebrated floating piano, an upright spinet that could have belonged to an old-time country church. With my index finger I softly touched a key that was yellow from age. A timid *ting* sang out. I examined the sheet music rack and cute brass pedals. I was surprised to discover the piano was not white—it was a very faint pink. Years ago, Dad had painted the mahogany wood white for better visibility onstage, but the wood was so dark it bled through and gave the piano the hue of a blushing maiden.

Something large and draped in black fabric was attached to the back of the piano. I assumed it was the mechanical device that made it rise. It was considerably taller than the piano, just as wide, and it hovered over the quaint spinet like its own distorted shadow. A chair was bolted to the piano. In each town, sponsors would be responsible for finding a local pianist to play it as it rose, turned in a circle, and landed. In old show days, they strapped the player to a little low-back chair. This time Dad had hired a metal worker to construct a chair with a tall canopy of grim bars to nearly encircle the pianist. He wanted to protect the player, still strapped to the chair, in case the apparatus malfunctioned onstage and the piano fell. In their years performing the trick, no injury or piano mishap had ever occurred, yet fears of a lawsuit hovered around the illusion. What it gained in safety, it lost in charm. The chair with its hood of bars was akin to an ugly throne from a futuristic draconian empire. Dad tried to soften its appearance by wrapping the bars and seat in sticky rattan-looking shelf paper. He wanted it to pass for an exotic wicker chair from the tropics. Instead, the little pink piano became even more of a curio.

The first day, after informing Dad that he was "a master at mechanics," Rick parted the black sheet and stepped inside to work on the piano. The clang of tools against metal pierced the quiet warehouse as we worked. The piano rose about one foot.

The rest of the show consisted of silver aluminum stands, tripods, black curtains, rickety hoists, metal rods, hobo suitcases, and old foulards so mice-nibbled we tossed them. There were large white, purple, red, and dark-blue boxes with black trim, and black boxes with bright chrome trim. Tables, pedestals, and a home-crafted cannon barrel. Everything rolled or should have rolled, except when wheels fell off. The entire show was like a scuffed-up fancy black shoe. The hardware holding the show together appeared to be in revolt: loose casters, screws, bolts, and hinges; little doors that wobbled; lids and doors that didn't open or close. The show's equipment needed sturdy joints, hardy spines and seams.

"What the show really needs," Dad said, looking at Clair and me, "is paint."

So, we painted. Every day after school, Mom took me to the warehouse, where Clair and I slapped black paint on every surface, while Mom sewed sequins and rhinestones on pants and shirts. Christmas was over and the countdown to our first show had begun: 38, 37, 36 days…Day after day, we ran out of time to rehearse. Finally, the day came.

"We'll do The Cannon," Dad announced.

We had cleared a small area for our provisional stage, bordered by show equipment and fairground clutter—exhibit stands, a hot dog vending cart, and signs that read Giant Geodes and Great American Bake-Off. It was cold in the warehouse, and we stood around with our hands stuffed in our jackets as pale winter light glared down on us from a stitch of high, dirty windows. The cousins pushed out the cannon with its cut-mirror barrel reflecting jagged, jittery light. Then they gripped each other's arms and braced for Mom's charge.

She hesitated on her launch pad and said apologetically, "Heavens to Betsy! I hate to do this to you boys!"

Then, fixing her gaze straight ahead, she ran. With their long arms Ben and Brody created a kind of basket to catch her, and, gathering speed, she leaped. They caught her with their matching brawn, lifted her off the ground, and loaded her feet first into the cannon barrel. There she went—legs, hips, torso, and head. Lastly, one soft pink hand scurried across the dark inside. The cousins and Dad flew around the cannon, rolling a hoist over and rigging up the barrel to a chain. Rick rolled the cannon base away, and the cannon hung free.

I'd seen an old show photo of The Cannon illusion. In a posed studio shot, an amusing drama had played out in black and white. Two men in dapper white jackets held my mother's straight-arrow body. In her little cuffed shorts and fishnet stockings, she was about to be shoved into the cannon mouth. Everyone shared big, giddy grins. A grand caper appeared to be underway. In the foreground, my father reigned as supreme mischief-maker in his dark tails and suppressed smile. He seemed to be saying, *I just can't help myself.* In the cold, grubby warehouse I saw none of that carefree revelry. The Cannon was just a clumsy game of pretend.

As the barrel was aimed upward, I sensed my mother was not inside it. Just then, as I turned toward the cannon base, the lid opened and I saw Mom's back. That's when I witnessed the secret motor of our magic show—box jumping. Her arms drew in, her shoulder blades rounded. The base was in the shape of an upside down "U," and her legs were down one side of the an upside down "U" and head and shoulders down the other. Dad had built it long ago exactly to her measurements with just enough jiggle room for her to get out, barely. She pushed up on her elbows and wiggled until the back of her head emerged. Her entire body was wrestling inside the jaws of an unyielding contraption. She strained, pushed, and squirmed, biting her lip, panting and withering as she freed one leg and then the other from the confining space. With her feet touching the ground only once, she promptly jumped into the trap of a mirror-trimmed black table.

For years, Dad had claimed to shoot my mother from a cannon on every poster, hanger, and banner. He also bragged to everyone that he had done so, and even nicknamed her the Human Cannonball. The trick, though, was only a flimsy suggestion of flight. Inside my pockets, I turned my cold hands into fists, embarrassed I had fallen for my father's P.T. Barnum assertions and sophisticated hokum. The crux of the entire illusion rested on my mother jumping lickety-split between two pieces of equipment.

The cousins placed a box on top of Mom's little hideout. Somehow she maneuvered herself from the table up through the trap into that box. The box was actually a nest of three boxes. The cousins removed one box from inside the other, and then, throwing back the lid of the last box, Mom stood up, cool and unruffled, the way I'd seen her after a trip to the grocery store. Ben and Brody grabbed her arms, and she was lowered to the ground. It appeared my mother did all the work. And in high heels.

At the warehouse we had no stage or backstage, and without these divisions the entire show was exposed on one flat open plane. I stood in the center of the chaotic array of equipment, with its secret orifices and shady nooks, considering the show's strange dusty magic and my mother's integral part in it.

Later on, Clair asked to see my textbooks so she could familiarize herself with my subjects. For a week I had been peeking at her over every odd box we painted. I found her fascinating. Her little gold earrings and her neat pearly fingernails, and the way she sat cross-legged on top of a crate to read a book and sip a diet soda. While she studied the table of contents of my algebra book, she played with her alphabet necklace. With book in hand, she had the earnestness of a librarian. She was about Cindy's age.

"Do you have a leather fringe jacket?" I suddenly asked. She briefly looked up. "Hmm, I used to."

She carried a canvas bag that read Wild Berries Food Co-op, featuring a drawing of a vegetable person with an apple for a head and carrots for arms and a broccoli hairdo. This bag held her teacher supplies, which included notebooks, No. 2 pencils, a clipboard, and for some reason an *M* encyclopedia.

Clair closed the book. "Do you need help with homework?" I told her no. I was still attending junior high, and we didn't leave for another month.

Ben and Brody headed our way. Suddenly, Clair and I were being inundated with *Saturday Night Live* and Steve Martin punch lines: "You wanna get small?" and "We're two wild and crazy guys!" Rick joined us and soon everyone was laughing except me. I felt sick. They were only there to pick up Clair for a walk to the snack bar outside the fairgrounds. My exclusion was so upsetting, my belly churned. Those old Katy Gwabel feelings had returned. I was afraid to speak. *Bwody, Wick, wha-ah you going?*

"Tomorrow bring your science book," Clair told me as they walked away.

Days passed at the chilly warehouse. We were bundled in jackets and hats, our fingers and noses still cold. Dismal gray light encapsulated us in drab ashen hues that never touched the magic show, nor its many confounding surfaces and gadgets with their own complicated density and vibrating mass. Each day there was a crisis, things lost or desperately needed, equipment not working. Rehearsals were stalled by half starts and wrong ways. The boys were often in differing postures of toil and weariness, hunched over, pounding on nails, tightening screws, or staring at their sneakers as they waited to be told what to do. Meanwhile, the piano was still grounded. Behind the drape, Rick's clanging tools sounded hollow and haphazard. The piano had been in storage so long it needed new parts, a cable, a rope. Sometimes it rose a few inches off the floor and quivered.

That night at home, Dad removed his Bee deck from his bedside table and practiced while I watched from the doorway. The cards fit into his hands similar to keys in a lock. He cascaded, flourished, fanned, and flung them. Cards climbed into the air, scaled and conquered it, then descended into nothing. This wasn't one of those cheesy pick-a-card tricks he was forced to do for company. This was a very old conversation he was having with their flat, waxy faces. His eyes remained focused on his reflection in his dresser mirror, hands straight and even as he watched the angles.

He glanced my way. "There you are!" he said with a smile of silver scaffolding.

Then he performed his original move—the One-Handed Card Production, unequaled even by Cardini. It was a swinging, swaying thing, a gentleman's swanky tease. With arms open wide, he flicked a card to his fingers and let it fall to the floor. Then he turned away and turned back. One arm opened again. Another card flicked to his fingers and floated to the floor. That's how it went, back and forth, an arm opening and closing, cards falling, a gallant one-arm waltz of a daffy wallflower. He was using one of his old decks, soft and creased, even the king cards weary and heavy-lidded.

Long ago, I had tried to play Crazy Eights with those cards, and my mother had snatched them out of my hands. "That's your father's manipulation deck." When I questioned her, she used her body, turning into Shiva with multiple undulating arms. "You know, sleight of hand, to music." I now understood what she was talking about. His card routine was a big and showy affair for folks in the balcony seats, not a close-up room.

As I watched him from my spot in the doorway, I flexed my fingers. My ten digits itched for those cards. I just wanted to touch them, inspect the pips and royal faces and cup them in my hand, even though my mother's message had been clear: *Don't touch your father's props.* I still remembered how they'd felt when I played Crazy Eights. Unlike other playing cards, Dad's cards were sticky. I later learned he used an old card-man's secret for a better grip. He rubbed them with a bar of dry soap.

The next night, I stationed myself at the doorway again. Dad removed a large pipe, almost two feet long, from a paisley flannel pillowcase. It had a round bowl and a long stem that gracefully curved as if from a painter's stroke. My thoughts were clicking. It was coming together. This was *The* Pipe. My parents had talked about The Pipe. It was a famed sleight-of-hand production so impressive that none of his brethren could figure out where he hid it on his body. He would pull this big calabash pipe out of *nowhere*. Crowds were known to cry out and applaud. It was the show's poetry and what set my father apart from the conjuring proletariat. Something about The Pipe cradled in his arms felt holy and hush-hush.

He slipped on his black tails over his Lee Grabel Realty slacks and rehearsed, first producing a bulldog, a corn cob, a billiard…a series of pipes that culminated with The Pipe, long, sinuous, uncoiling. Just a skip in time, and it popped up in his arms. He knew how to maximize the finale. Bringing it to his lips, he winked at the crowds in the mirror.

Afterward, I sat on the edge of their bed next to The Pipe. A quick inspection told me it wasn't a real pipe. The tobacco hole was a square piece of black tape spotted with metallic copper paint to resemble burning embers. This was a dummy pipe, handcrafted by my father. The mouthpiece was from a real pipe, hacked off and attached to the stem with neatly wound black duct tape. The long stem of The Pipe appeared soft and rubbery. Later, I figured out it was a car radiator hose. And its round, bulbous bowl he carved himself out of basswood and stained dark cherry. As an aside, there is no film of this particular illusion. On the occasions that my father knew the routine would be filmed, he intentionally left it out. He feared someone might discover how he produced The Pipe by playing the tape forward and in reverse.

Suddenly, Dad appeared next to me with the whisper of pipes on his fingers. He slipped The Pipe back into its pillowcase and the other pipes into their cases. Perhaps rehearsal was over, or perhaps I had been looking too long. Not only was I forbidden to touch my father's props, but it was also wrong for me to study them, be curious, or ask questions about a trick's inner workings.

I'd come this far only to discover that my complicity was limited in the magic show. Apparently, there were inner sanctums within inner sanctums. Still, it was impossible to believe I was an outlier of this adventure. My father's magic was my magic, his dream was my dream, and together we'd claim all the starlit stages of Vegas as our own.

Back in my bedroom that night, I kept the record player off and sang a cappella once again. The dictionary defined "a cappella" as "without instrumental accompaniment." So unlike the magic show with its forty-foot truck, geese, fake women's feet, nails, cannon barrel, and flat black paint by the gallons. A magic show wasn't something we could carry with us. It was too big to fit inside a gold locket dangling over a heart, and it could never be reduced to a poem scribbled on paper and stuffed in a pocket.

I stood in front of my mirror and posed the way the assistants did in those old show photos. With arms behind me, hands clasped, and one knee bent, I pasted a vacuous smile across my blemished face. It didn't allow for much spontaneity. Certainly no singing or dancing. Moreover, I had no lines in the show. My presence onstage would be cast in complete silence. In the mirror, I tugged up my bra strap and studied my budding new figure with its contours, valleys, and chambers. Since starting my period, I had been sprouting new flesh everywhere. It made our two young male assistants all the more interesting to me. Fun boys, fitful workers, prone to distant, bored looks when not busy, walking around with screwdrivers sticking out of the back pockets of their Levi's.

Each morning I got Brody's "Brace Face" greeting as he jostled my hair.

That night in my bedroom, I could still feel his hands on my head, shaking my thoughts into a new order. He had been so close I had seen the acne on his chin, and the searing light from his rambunctious smile.

The next day, Dad wanted Brody to be featured in The Backstage. The premise of the illusion was to give the audience a "backstage view" of how an illusion worked. Except it had a surprise ending. Brody. After tricking the audience into thinking a female would be produced from the box, it would be him.

We stood around looking at the equipment for The Backstage. Two large red and blue boxes with shiny black trim, side by side, were attached to a black platform with two deep, covert traps within its innermost body.

"You have to do something when you appear," Dad urged Brody. "Funny. For a laugh."

I expected a dumb forced gag for his big production, so I was surprised to see Brody inspired as he jumped up on the contraption to show us. Tilting back his head, he dramatically reached for a comb in his back pocket and swiped it through his red-brown hair. Then, looking up, he jumped, startled to see the crowd there.

We burst out laughing. It was perfect. I gulped. My heart was loose and swaying from a string. I kept glancing at him, suddenly too self-conscious to look long.

That was the last time I ever saw his funny pose. I ended up being the girl in the trick. This meant when he appeared to the crowd, I was hidden away in the trick's hollowed bottom, a trap ungraced by black paint, only knotty wood grain. In the coming towns we played, I would hear only creaking boards as Brody stood above me, making the crowd laugh and applaud. My curled fetal form, adorned in dark eyeshadow and sateen, lay under his feet, a princess exiled to the underworld.

9

MARITAL DISCORD
RIGHT ON TIME

The Clocks routine

FOUR WEEKS BEFORE OUR first show, Dad received a call from Rick's father, who said Rick had been arrested for not paying alimony. The next morning, Dad placed another newspaper ad and hired Danny, a stocky man with short legs, a beefy chest, and a salt-and-pepper beard trimmed to a sharp point below his chin. He used to truck staging for an evangelical revival show, and on his round splotchy bicep there was a tattoo of Moses shaking his staff and parting the sea.

"We have to get that piano rising," Dad briefed him on the first day, and they stepped behind the black drape to confer.

Clanging tools rang through the warehouse. At one point, Danny walked out, grabbed a big wrench from the tool kit, and hurried back inside. More clanging. The spinet rose one foot, shook a little, and stopped.

The next morning, Danny called and quit the show, citing a family crisis. Our first show was coming up in less than thirty days, and we still had no trusty truck driver and piano caretaker.

Mom lowered her eyebrows. "You have to call Al," she insisted.

Al was a close and loyal friend, and if asked he would come. He was also unhappy at his new job managing a trailer park.

Dad refused. "I'll put another ad in the newspaper."

She turned away in silent protest. Around the crew she feigned a smile, but with us she succumbed to gloom, one brow arching at Dad's slightest remark. To her, our series of roadies was an ominous sign that our magical tour was heading for calamity.

Meanwhile, Dad had set up the clocks for his new routine. Clocks the size of bedside alarms, baseballs, and beach balls—and three as tall as a toddler—reigned over the living room. With their shiny silver bodies and exaggerated white-and-black-numbered faces, they were the timepieces of clowns, fake and hollow, something slapped on a wrist for laughs, except Mom wasn't laughing.

"When will we rehearse *that?*" she said, nodding her head toward the little army of ticking time.

"We'll get to it," Dad assured her, even though time was running out.

The next day, when we rehearsed The Vanishing Horse, our pretty mare Frankie refused to walk inside the contraption. Halfway up the ramp, she stopped, neighed, and wagged her head. We tried three times. The ceiling of the Flora Dora was too low for her. My mind snapped shut. No, it couldn't be true that the illusion was irreparably flawed. I watched Frankie's swishing tail as Ben led her out of the warehouse and back to her horse trailer. Everything about Frankie was perfect for our show. She wasn't too big or small, about fifteen hands, with a sweet, gentle temperament. All the same, she shared a horse's sensitivity and was easily spooked.

Everyone wandered away, not knowing what else to do, while I stayed by the suddenly worthless equipment, a mourner too shocked to move from a casket.

Across the way, Mom's fingers on her mouth could not hide her stricken face. This disaster added to her worries. We were under contractual obligation to bring sponsors a vanishing-horse illusion. Dad would have to call Mr. Bly with the bad news and then call a lawyer. I glanced at him. He slowly paced, rubbing the corners of his mouth. What was going on? His eyes were cast down, unseeing, thoughts moving across his forehead. Then I knew. He was designing a new horse illusion as a replacement. Just then his chin lifted as if the answer lay in the presumed nothingness of air. He grabbed his yellow tablet to formulate. I heard his scratching pen.

He called the crew over. "Okay, kids, this is what we'll do."

The new trick would be simple. Onstage we would carry two panels, creating a four-wall "barn." Ben would lead Frankie into the "barn." One panel would conceal Ben and Frankie in the front, the other in the sides and back. Ben would simply lead her out through an exit in the back panel, then through the curtain split in the backdrop and offstage. When we dropped the panels onstage, Frankie and Ben would be gone.

"It's hokey, but it'll work," Dad said.

It didn't matter if it was hokey, as long as it prevented legal trouble in five states. Dad scribbled out what we needed: fourteen yards of fabric, one dozen two-by-fours, a commercial-grade staple gun, and little finishing nails.

By the end of the day, we had a new illusion. Ben held Frankie's bridle as he walked her through it. The whispering panels assembled and reassembled around her, then her swift and easy exit. The entire trick was about two minutes. Across the warehouse, the Flora Dora had been pushed away, reclassified as unwanted bric-a-brac.

Next to the glass-studded cannon barrel, Mom sewed rhinestones on costumes with a downturned mouth. I gritted my teeth, annoyed she couldn't acknowledge the successes of the day.

In a few days we welcomed Owen, a thin, wiry man who used to haul iron out of Pittsburgh. On his first day, he jumped into his duties with enthusiasm, his long limbs in constant motion. Then Dad led him to the covered piano.

"Don't you worry, Mr. G. I'll have her rising every night like the moon," he said, and, parting the drape, he stepped inside.

Not long after, it happened. The piano began a breathtaking ascent. Dad pulled the drape away so he could move around it. A large metal frame extended out of the piano. On the back of the piano was a big gear with a chain around it, and at the far end Owen turned a crank wheel. A cable slowly moved around the frame, which lifted a large metal arm attached to the piano. When it was about five feet off the ground, Owen turned a side crank and the spinet rotated in a circle. The large chain slowly moved around the big gear in the back of the piano.

Dad studied the chain. "It's tracking," he said.

"Gotcha, Mr. G," Owen followed.

The entire crew stopped their tasks to watch. As the piano turned in the air, the board behind the keys fell away and Dad grabbed it. I could see the little wooden hammers and steel strings of the harp. It turned completely upside down, then slowly upright again and landed with the ease of an angel bearing good news. We must have sensed the show was finally coming together, and we burst out clapping. We'd been working at the warehouse for nearly a month, and we were bored with the routine and eager for the tour.

Except Mom.

We had three weeks before our first show, and the clock routine was still unrehearsed. Dad described it as a *show-off number*, his chance to display the finesse and skills he valued most as a showman. His excitement left my mother unmoved. For months, Dad had sealed himself in the garage, soldering the clocks' round bodies from aluminum and cutting little clock hands from black stickers. Now a bevy of eighteen clocks filled our living room. On the floor, sofa, and coffee table, their round white faces were fraught by the symbol of time. Mom tried to ward them off with frequent unfriendly glances.

As our first show on February 7th approached, The Clocks rose to the top of Dad's yellow list. Driving back from the warehouse one night, he told Mom, "Tonight we start."

Learning the clock routine would be a herculean task for my mother. It demanded military precision, moves as smooth and flawless as a thief's. While my father winked and pranced for the crowd, she was to be the workhorse of the routine, two steps behind him, slipping him a heap of metal as easily as passing a saltshaker.

Dad set up for the routine in their bedroom before a full-length mirror while I sat in the doorway to watch. In the center was a T-shaped table covered in soft black felt and trimmed in silver that Dad had crafted himself. As he explained the trick to Mom, it soon became clear she had to surreptitiously remove clocks, some quite large, from hidden compartments in the T-table and pass them to him concealed in bundles of silks.

"The audience is gonna know it's me," she cautioned. "They'll see I'm giving you everything."

"They'll be looking at me," he said, pointing his thumb at himself.

"Pfft," she loudly exhaled. "You always say that."

Dad figured if he hammed it up, the audience would not be distracted by Mom's sneaking him those clocks.

The finale was the hardest. She had to carry, one at a time, three big clocks concealed in silks, and she had to do it without revealing their weight, walking upright and lightly. Two clocks were almost three feet high and more than eighteen inches across.

"Lift it up," Dad said, referring to one of the big clocks.

She slipped her fingers into the ring at the top of the clock and stepped forward. Her entire body leaned to one side. She pursed her lips. "That's heavy."

They started to practice and soon discovered additional challenges. Mom had to hand him every clock in time to each ringing bell recorded within the music.

Dad wanted to fool the crowd into thinking the clocks were real. As each clock was produced from a bundle of foulards, a bell sounded. He had actually walked through the entire routine by himself many times so that he knew the exact moment each clock had to be produced. Then he went to a sound engineer and added bells to the routine music at those exact times. However, in order to create this effect, Mom had to keep up with the ringing bells in the music. Timing was so important that if she was late retrieving one clock, it threw the entire routine out of sync. If she was early handing him a clock, they had to stall. Both of them had to move as one, every step matched with the other.

It went wrong right away. Mom couldn't get the clocks out of the T-table in time, and the silks gaped open, revealing white oval faces. Dad floundered without his loads in a clumsy dance. As she lurched forward, he pawed the air behind him and cried, "Where are you?" They fumbled over the exchanges, two hapless clods.

When one of the big clocks knocked against her legs, he barked, "It's this way."

Gripping the silks in one hand to cover the table, he pulled the big clock out from its slender little compartment and walked forward. It wasn't easy for him either.

"You're stronger than me," she remarked and opened her hands. Her fingers were red from the small ring handles on the clocks. "They pinch me."

He shrugged it off. "You'll get used to it."

She started passing him clocks with the attitude of a fed-up waitress carelessly slapping down club sandwiches to a rude diner. Meanwhile, Dad mugged it up for the mirror, producing a clock with a two-step and a flourish. For the finale, Mom relinquished all pretense by grabbing the largest clock and oafishly dragging it to him.

Her lack of artifice shocked him. "What are you doing?!" he implored.

She dropped the clock, and it fell over on its face. She crossed her arms and scowled. "This routine just might not work. Have you thought of that?"

An impenetrable shroud fell across his face. Abandoning the old horse illusion was easier because it was a flash and spectacle number. Conversely, The Clocks was all artistry, a holy marriage of skill and style. It also had marketable appeal. "We have to do it," Dad told her, his breath ragged. "It's perfect for the casino lounges."

Her eyes darkened. Something had gone terribly awry. Her fingers were red, and the clocks lay on the floor, an elite military squad, fallen.

At my post in the doorway, I bit my lip and waited for what would happen next. I was dismayed at how quickly the rehearsal had devolved. I sensed their fight was less about the routine than Mom's feeling forced into this farfetched crusade. It stirred up old marital complaints.

Mom's mouth tightened. "You never think about me."

"You hate it when I try something new," he answered.

That's when I left for the television set downstairs. At the end of the night, passing by their room, I saw that the entire rehearsal had stopped. They were facing each other in differing poses of distress in a sea of big white oval faces. The music with the annoying ringing bells had, mercifully, stopped.

Mom complained about an expensive new bill from an insurance carrier. The sponsors wanted our "amazing illusions" adequately insured.

"Just to hang a woman upside down at a piano," she told him. "Don't you feel a little foolish?"

In the coming days, my parents would rehearse the routine at home as the warehouse lacked the mirrors necessary for Dad to scrutinize his moves. Each evening, with the enthusiasm of ballplayers filing onto the field of a losing game, they would retire to their bedroom, a maelstrom of clocks, silks, trays, and tables. Then the music would kick in, and those shrill ringing bells consumed our house. Each time I passed their bedroom, clocks appeared without bells, bells rang without clocks. They were graceless solo acts.

One night when heading upstairs to my room, I heard Mom say, "Do you think the school district is really going to let Katy go?"

I froze on the steps. She actually hoped my inability to go would subvert the tour.

The next night, I found her throwing down blankets on the sofa in the living room. I could hardly speak.

"What are you doing?" I sputtered.

"I'm sleeping down here," she snapped.

Dad called out, "Helen, come to bed!" He stood at the foot of the stairs in his green-striped pajamas, poking a cotton swab in his ear. "You're being unreasonable!"

Mom clutched her pillow. "I'm not going up there!"

Mom's parents' sixtieth wedding anniversary party was during the tour. Mom had told Dad and Mr. Bly not to book any shows that weekend in May so she could fly to Oklahoma. Mom had just discovered they had booked the weekend anyway. We were scheduled to play Ridgecrest, California, on May 6th, the night of my grandparents' big anniversary party at Eischen's Bar in Okarche, Oklahoma.

For many nights, I had found solace in my bedroom by cranking up my record player so as not to hear their bickering, but this disruption of sleeping arrangements I couldn't shut out. I touched my stomach, feeling queasy.

Cupping her cheek in her hand, Mom lay down on her makeshift bed, slowly—leg, elbow, cheek. "He just does what he wants," she mewed. Through her gown, I saw one pointy hip bone, a lonely protrusion in a sea of powder blue.

Her powerlessness in this situation had finally toppled her, struck her down with a flu of the heart and sent her early to bed. I remembered a few years earlier when our trio was at a restaurant eating dinner. Mom and I started to sing the jingle from a candy bar commercial. We were laughing when Dad put his finger to his lips. "Shhhh." Singing at a table was bad manners. He was cranky from another harried day at the office, and his cheeks were stuffed with sourdough bread from the basket on the table. Despite our annoyance, we shut up.

Walking up the steps to my bedroom, I lay down on my bed, and felt the blips and beats of my heart. I thought of my mother's crushed saddened figure downstairs. And then I thought of the magic show's tables and boxes in lustrous black and midnight patina, all its mercurial chrome edges, and the hope it harbored in its silent silken maneuvering.

Dad was right. Mom was being unreasonable. To be a Las Vegas headliner was the only dream, it was all that mattered, more than money, time, or family. I wanted fans and flattery, blood-red roses thrown on a stage at my feet.

She had to learn The Clocks. Dad couldn't do it without her. We couldn't do the show without her. She had to perk up and quit complaining.

Shhhh.

10

∝∾

RULES OF THE ROAD

The traveling magic show, 1950s

ONLY ONE THING WOULD save our dream. A home for Mom in
Vegas where she could cook beef tenderloin, grow red hibiscus, and
decorate the living room in green, yellow, and salmon. As the clock
rehearsals continued, I determined this to be the only solution to my
parents' disparate needs.

I imagined a house of cool white stucco with a palm tree in the
yard somewhere near the strip. At night, we'd eat our dinners on trays
in front of the television, and then jump into the Cadillac for our
performance at the Sahara, the Stardust, the Sands...

When I wasn't thinking about that white stucco house, I rumi-
nated on my parents' story about The Broom Suspension. When they
were younger, they had rehearsed this illusion in a cousin's garage.
As this was before the invention of plastic, a metal harness dug into
Mom's ribs as her body rose at a right angle from the broom. As
preparation for the stage, she had to conceal her discomfort behind a
tranquil face.

While Dad practiced his mumbo jumbo finger-flutter antics, Mom would finally croak, "Hurry up," to which he would respond, "Look natural."

A fight usually ensued. At one point, they had considered divorce. *Divorce.* Perhaps the clock rehearsal was a forewarning of what was to come.

One night our trio left the warehouse early for dinner. After we scooted into a booth at a local restaurant, my parents buried their heads in the menus to avoid looking at each other. Under the table I clamped my palms together to squeeze out the tension. Our heralded trio had become just another family without anything to say. I didn't realize how much I missed our silly jesting. I needed it to offset my lack of friends at school. I usually spent lunchtime hiding in the library so no one would see me eating alone. At our table I fiddled with the spoon, its empty, joyless face staring back at me.

I recalled years earlier when we were at the Oakland airport. Mom and I were flying to Oklahoma, and Dad had waited with us for our plane. My parents had been affectionate that day, with little jokes, hugs, and pats on the shoulder. Seeing him walk toward us across the terminal, Mom had tilted her head and said in a soft, dewy voice, "Lee's such a handsome man."

Before we walked onto the plane, they hugged and kissed on the mouth. Mom patted his cheek and said, "You sweet guy." My young mind could not wrap around the complexities of adult relationships, and my parents' tight knot of love and anger.

Before things improved, the house got really quiet. The bickering and menacing music stopped and a shaky silence moved in. And the clocks disappeared. Dad lugged them to the garage and at night, after the warehouse rehearsal, he worked on them while Mom sat in front of the television with a can of cashews as if recovering from a dreadful malady. Then one night the music started again.

Dad had modified the routine for Mom. He'd enlarged the clock rings so that they would not squeeze her fingers. Dad also agreed that the audience would be suspicious of Mom's part, so he'd devised more misdirection with a zombie ball, which is a ball that dances along the edge of a large open foulard. Except instead of a ball, he'd made a clock. The foulard would help conceal some of Mom's actions behind him. Once the clock rehearsal started again, they practiced intently every evening.

At some point, I migrated back to their bedroom to watch from the doorway again. The entire routine was one big orchestrated dance with their covert and overt moves so intertwined as to be impercep-tible. Each time Dad reached back, she was there to take his clock. Each time Mom passed him a foulard, his hand was waiting to accept it. Their moves were in time with each other, and the clock produc-tions in time to the bells, an original and perfect dance wrought from the same marital teamwork that had built their lives together.

From my post in the doorway, my spirit lifted. The ordeal was over. Mom raised her chin and swayed a little to the music, while Dad hammed it up just for me, bending down to tickle a clock out from behind my ear. My mouth curved in a smile. Our trio was back. I hadn't known we were so fragile.

The night before we left for our first show in Fairfield, we ate at a Chinese restaurant with the crew. A tent sign by the front door adver-tised a drink called the Chartreuse Moose.

"Come on, order it," Dad urged us with his new smile. His teeth had been freed of metal, and now they were too large and almost as white as his hair. He might have frisked a movie star for them. "I dare someone to order the Chartreuse Moose," he teased, eyes dancing.

We exchanged amused glances and chuckled. Each time a waiter left the bar, we eyed their tray to see if he carried a drink that resem-bled a Chartreuse Moose.

Dad told us the route of the magic show tour. We would start in Fairfield, a little way from home, then crisscross northward through the Pacific Northwest, turn right at the Canadian border, and do a loop around central Washington. Then we'd head to Idaho, where we'd curve southward. After a mad showless dash across Nevada, we'd start again in Northern California. There we would head south, leapfrogging from city to city along the Central Valley, capped off with a few high desert towns. We had one show in Barstow to gather our wits before the long trek across the Mojave Desert to our show at the convention center in Las Vegas on May 2nd. After that it was almost over. Only a scattering of towns off Highway 101 back up to the San Francisco area. Our first date was February 7th and our last, May 23rd. We would be gone a total of 107 days. Three months and eighteen days. Almost four months.

"We *have* to keep on schedule," Dad said. "It's a Rule of the Road."

The schedule dictated that after each show, we'd load the equip-ment into the truck and drive to the next town. The following day we would unload the truck, do the show, and then load the truck up again before traveling to the next town.

"It's called one-nighters," he said. "Do you know one-nighters?" His head swiveled back and forth, up and down the table, looking at each one of us.

We all shook our heads, except for Mom.

He cleared his throat. "It's the most grueling touring of all," he told us. "To do them, we have to be fast."

Owen nodded his head as if he understood speed deep in his bones. He spun boxes fast, broke down the piano fast, walked faster than Dad. "I gotcha, Mr. G," he said with approval.

Dad leaned forward on his arms and eyed the cousins. "That means right after the show, you must have all crates packed and ready to be loaded out," he ordered. "It's a Rule of the Road."

I wondered how many rules there were.

"We have to be out of the theater by eleven o'clock." He karate-chopped the air. "*By eleven*," he insisted. "If we get behind, the worst thing could happen." His eyes were as clear as rainwater. We waited. Mom shifted in her seat next to me.

"We could miss a show," he stated grimly. He warned of contractual violations, money loss, damaged reputation, and possible lawsuits. And other hazards of the road: body injuries, hospitalizations, fatigue, food poisoning, loneliness, stress, germs...

He scanned the table. "Did you all get tetanus shots?"

We squinted at each other. No, we said.

He slowly inhaled, pained by the air filling his chest. "Listen," he said. "On a tour of one-nighters, the towns and theaters change but not the people you travel with. The waitresses, motel clerks, and sponsors will change"—he raised his finger for emphasis—"but not us. *Look around you*. We will be the only people you will have contact with for four months." We gazed down at our hands and the paper placemats and not at each other. "All personal grievances must be set aside for the sake of the show. It's a Rule of the Road." His penetrating eyes swept over us. "Our biggest challenge will be each other."

His cautionary remarks went unheeded. Down the table, the boys' windswept expressions implied a gale of chance had blown them to our show. Clair intently drained her tea bag around a spoon. Owen, however, was energized by my father's entreaty, his wide eyes glued to him as he described our high-speed traveling crucible with farm animals. Next to me, Mom's silence felt thick and heavy.

A waiter glided by with a blended drink in a bulbous glass, bar fruit stacked on the rim. We turned our heads. It was pale green tinged in neon yellow, something squeezed out of a dying lawn.

Dad excitedly pointed at the drink. "See? That's what the road does to you. Turns you into a Chartreuse Moose!" His laughter was contagious, and we joined him, confident all the blunders in the world would never touch us.

At home that night, I packed my suitcase. I was bringing a two-hundred-page, five-tab notebook as my journal, as well as the little purple notebook. Most exciting was a little black sequin bag. It was a fitting possession for a daughter of a Vegas headliner, and I had nagged Mom into buying it. Inside I stashed a compact of smoky eyeshadow, blood-red rouge, and a mascara case of discotheque metallic silver.

By the time I was done packing, I felt free from Alamo, drifting away from everything familiar before we even walked out the door. I floated one of my mother's scarves over my record player. Maybe we'd be gone longer than four months. I secretly hoped this tour would lead me to my own career in show business. How exactly this would happen, I had no idea. I just believed my father's magic show would somehow trigger a confluence of events that would catapult me into fame. In many ways, I was already a rising star, even though the show was not what I imagined. Messy, disorganized, arduous. And not very magical.

III

The Great Houdini up in the Sky

⁓

My dear boy, you have my sincere good wishes…
and sympathy.

—Howard Thurston to Dante, 1910,
upon learning he was embarking on his first world tour

11

THE ONE AND ONLY,
THE GREAT LEE GRABEL

As far as i no it's going to be "show time" for the rest of my teens.

Lee and Katy, the aspiring star

IN FAIRFIELD, MY INVISIBLE crowds were replaced by almost three hundred real folks. Peeking through the curtain before the show, I saw one big clamoring mass of pink faces. My stage fright came on strong, an outbreak of nerves deep in my stomach. After all my singer fantasies on vast, star-specked stages, I couldn't believe how shaky I felt. Clammy, cardiac-thumping fear, a sweeping case of jitters. I squeezed my fingers in a vise grip. With only a few dress rehearsals before we left, I felt we were unprepared. The audience could roll their eyes, laugh at us, or walk out. We also didn't have a proper stage. It was a high school gym, and we'd had to assemble our own proscenium, a portable stage draped in black velour, a stage without real walls, about four feet off the ground. Before the show, I had walked into the gym and studied it from a distance. The Broadway Magical Mystery Extravaganza had been shrunk and stuffed into a cube shrouded in black between two basketball hoops. Rows of metal chairs ran across the court from one free-throw line to the other.

Showtime was near, and it was time to dress. As we didn't have a proper dressing room, we arranged our wardrobe trunks in a circle and hung a big foulard for privacy. For The Opening, Clair and I dressed in black leotards and black-and-white-striped vests edged in rhinestones. We tied black chiffon scarves around our necks in smart little bows and slipped on black pumps. I heard children romping and squealing through the curtains. Suddenly, a little hand reached under the curtain by my shoe. Mom was there in a flash. "Shoo!" she cried. The proscenium afforded the little kiddos a perfect height to torment us. The curtain lifted and a delighted bug-eyed devil was laughing at us. "Get! Get!" Mom said, flailing her arms and stamping a foot. We were being overrun by children, rowdy, boisterous children. I was stunned by how many there were. For a cosmopolitan show for adults, the Broadway Magical Mystery Extravaganza apparently attracted a lot of kids. Dad flagged down a sponsor by the bleachers, and soon nice men in Kiwanis vests stationed themselves around the perimeter of the stage to protect us from their mischief.

Mom started the preshow music, and a din of synthesizers and guitars bounced around the gym in acoustic bedlam. Six doves in a wire cage cooed as Clair and I removed four of them, snapping them into black quilted covers and placing them on top of Dad's wardrobe trunk. Mom wore a long, clingy dress trimmed in shimmering black sequins that shed and pooled on her table like bits of black sugar. Before the show, I had seen her vigorously tease her hair to give it volume. It was now artfully styled into an impressive mass of airy gossamer.

Across the way, the cousins admired each other in their laser-blue dress shirts with such frilly ruffled bibs it gave them the appearance of puffed-up birds. At Mom's table, I applied and reapplied my lipstick in a little hand mirror she kept on the amplifier. Behind the closed curtain, the big gold top hat was positioned center stage in still, empty space.

At his trunk, Dad added his final accessories: cummerbund, sapphire sequin vest, black bow tie. And one more item. From the top drawer of his wardrobe trunk, he removed a gold medal on a bright-red ribbon. He draped it around his neck so that it dangled slightly below his black bow tie for all to see. It was an ornate gilded medal in the shape of a cross with etched words from a group of magicians from Texas, honoring him for his years on the road in 1958. He then slipped on his black tuxedo jacket and placed the four pouched doves in four strategic pockets.

He paced and rehearsed his opening lines. "So many fine people here tonight. Hello, sir. Hello, ma'am." He then blew so forcefully out of his mouth it sounded like a horse flapping its lips. "Hhhhhhsssssssjjjjjj." This was his mouth exercise for better word enunciation onstage. He continued to pace, practicing his patter and vibrating, wagging, and flailing his lips. "Hhhhhhsssssssjjjjjj! So many fine people here tonight. Hello there, sir. When did you get out of jail? Hhhhhhsssssssjjjjjj!"

Through the curtain, the audience clamored, the music blared. His step quickened, his voice rose until the backstage could not contain him, not his throbbing body, nor his gurgling, erupting words. He turned toward the backstage door where he would walk around the gym to the front for his grand appearance behind the audience. He began all shows this way, and he considered this his signature entrance.

Before he left, Mom stopped him. Wrapping him in a dense cloud of wafting hairspray, she delicately leaned forward and softly said, "Lee, do you have everything?"

He jumped. His hands frisked his body, sweeping, patting, and tapping on his pockets here and there. Then he was gone.

I took my position onstage with the crew. Clair and I stood on both sides of the hat, and the cousins and Owen stood three in a row behind us. Facing the closed curtain, we silently waited, listening to the sounds of the crowd. I quickly glanced at Clair, who stared ahead, pale and motionless. She was as spooked by the big crowd as I was. My faith in my father took a dive. America's Leading Magician of the 1950s. The 1950s were a long time ago!

A recording of a man's voice boomed over the speakers. "The Broadway Magical Mystery Extravaganza! With America's leading showman, the one and only, the Great Lee Grabel!" A circus-y trombone blared.

I heard Dad greeting his audience from the back of the gym. "What fine people here tonight. How are you, sir? Does your probation officer know you're here?" A round of rollicking laughter. "Hello, ma'am. Don't you look lovely tonight! Nice dye job."

He was walking down the aisle, heading our way. The crowd rumbled as grand symphonic music kicked in over the speakers. I stared at the closed curtain and braced myself. It swooshed open. My smile of jumbled wire twinkled. Dad leaped up the steps, waving his top hat and red silk, illuminated by a blaze of blue-white spotlight so strong it created an astral halo around his head.

Those first moments onstage were a dream, fluttering doves and flapping silks, Dad prancing around with doves on his finger. The spotlight was so blinding I couldn't see the crowd and didn't know what they thought of us. I felt sweaty under the arms. Dad feigned a clumsy trip across the stage. A playful bit of misdirection that allowed him to slip his hand in his tuxedo jacket for that fourth dove reveal. A small burst of applause shimmied through the crowd. They liked us. A surge of confidence broadened my smile.

The Opening was a series of tricks and illusions, a kind of hit-and-run magic all over the stage. Although we each had our own duties, we had to move as one—one body, one beast, with many arms and legs. While our male crew stood behind waiting for their cues, Mom held the dove tray, Clair handed him a net, and I retrieved a dove, holding it tight as I hurried offstage. For one instant in the wings, I had this sense of rushing bodies and being caught between dark and tremendous light.

When I think back it still feels surreal to me, our faces drenched in white light and powder, the blaring music, the resplendent silks that tumbled from my father's top hat, all his jolly prancing amid the flutter of snowy white doves. I find it astounding I was even there, that I was at one time onstage smiling vacuously amid all that ballyhoo. I remember the spotlight most of all, its heat and ferocious force. The way the spotlight followed my father everywhere, upstage, downstage, and to the top center step, where he showered the audience with dimpled smiles and winks. I wondered if the spotlight was really following him, or was he following the spotlight?

Out of a bundle of foulards, Dad produced a big white goose. It craned its neck to and fro and parted its bright yellow beak into a loud and definite *cronk*, prompting the crowd to applaud once they knew it was real. Two more geese were revealed. Their big white bodies had a deep pearly sheen in the spotlight, and they waddled around on their webbed feet before being snatched up by Ben and Brody. Then Dad darted over to the hat, pulling out big colorful foulards and then cages of tropical birds. Macaws, cockatoos, and parrots of ratty, tattered foam in faded yellow, blue, and red were flourished before the crowd in collapsible wire cages.

Backstage, I prepared for my big production: jumping out of the top hat. I crouched down in the wings at the edge of the curtain. When Owen and Brody held up a banner reading "Grabel" across the stage, Ben carried the top hat off its pedestal and paraded it up and down to show folks it was empty. My cue. From backstage, I ran behind the banner and squatted down on the pedestal. As the top hat was lowered down on me, I parted the bottom lip of the hat. I was inside. The banner was taken away, and Ben rolled the hat downstage. I knew Dad was near when the spotlight spilled inside, turning my kneecaps white.

He called my name and it amplified through the gym, "Kate!"

I jumped up.

Blinding light hit me. Strong hands gripped my waist, lifted me up, and set me onstage to a round of applause. My heart thundered. A glorious fervor overtook me. Past the spotlight, I could feel the eyes of a breathing crowd. *Behold my splendor!* I bowed in the light.

I was to learn that light didn't really belong to me. In my father's show I would be the lone dim figure holding a tray or a coin bucket in the dregs of his spotlight, but jumping out of that hat would always be mine. In many cold and cavernous theaters in strange towns, I would come to crave jumping out of that hat for that one moment when no one looked at my father—they looked at me.

During the show I stationed myself in the wings and was soon riding high on Lee Grabel's legerdemain. He unlinked big silver rings with his breath, escaped knots tied by two husky men, and hoodwinked little boys. He crushed a man's watch and burned another's dollar bill and restored them both. Clocks dangled from his fingers and coins scaled sheer, immutable light. He produced that big calabash pipe as he strolled and teased, then he tongued a cigarette. He called kids onstage to help with the tricks and always misread their gender, calling little girls with short hair "boys," and boys with long hair "girls." He pulled a sausage out of a poor guy's shirt and said, "Sorry to have exposed your lunch!" People laughed, hollered, and pointed. When Dad elevated that white piano off the stage floor, a dormant power had finally awakened and spilled from his hands. I melted into sappy gratitude when raucous applause filled the gym.

At the end of The Cannon, Mom was lifted out of that box and Dad introduced her: "Helene!" The spotlight latched onto them, two dazzling diamonds in a burglar's glove. Linking hands, they bowed, looking better than they ever did at the Rotary Club Christmas party.

The spotlight was so powerful Dad couldn't see the audience, so he developed a way of looking through the light as if speaking to individuals. He would say, "Look a little closer, young man." He pretended to make eye contact with people he could not see. "Ma'am, you see this card? Now it's gone." Folks thought he was speaking directly to them, and he captured their attention for the entire show, both the first and second half, covering more than two hours.

In The Substitution Trunk, Mom and Dad switched places in a locked trunk, and Mom had to get him out with the help of volunteers. As the men stood around the trunk, Mom, wearing a tight red jumpsuit, passed out keys to little locks. I watched one man ogle her cleavage as she sashayed around issuing orders, a sexy sergeant in a boned bodice.

At intermission Dad charged backstage and lamented, "Two kids had their backs to me talking the entire show."

Mom nodded sympathetically as he sat down in a chair behind his wardrobe trunk. His eyes were outlined in black and his face was caked with makeup. His black tuxedo gleamed, an animal skin in the faint light. He didn't fit backstage anymore. He was a creature of the spotlight, who still belonged to his waiting crowd just beyond the curtain.

In the second half, The Floating Ball went awry. Rigged across the stage was a wire that ran through eyelets of a shiny silver metallic ball. Each time Dad cast the ball across the stage, it whined on the wire. *Shrzzzzzzzzz.* A murmur ran through the gym. It sounded identical to a toy monorail. "Shrzzzzzzzz" went the ball. "Shrzzzzzz" went the kids. Their knack for imitation was quite impressive. I stood backstage, horrified. I wished Dad would cut the number short. All night the kids had been waiting for a mistake, and now they had found it.

At the end of the show, I took a deep breath and walked toward Dad's wardrobe trunk. Obviously, he didn't know the audience had heard it. As he unclipped his bow tie, I politely broke the bad news about his noisy floating ball.

He waved the remark away with his hand. "Oh, they can't hear it," he said, clearly unconcerned.

I walked away, baffled. Little boys leaving the theater were still making that sound.

In each town, the sponsors were required to arrange for movers to help load and unload the truck. Usually one of the sponsors would volunteer their son and his sports team. Throughout the tour, high school varsity or junior varsity boys moved us in and out in exchange for free tickets to the show. After the show, the boy-movers were not allowed on the stage until everything was packed in its crates.

In Fairfield, boys from the high school basketball team in letterman jackets overran the stage, maneuvering boxes on dollies and rolling them to the truck. The truck was packed like a puzzle, each crate, spray-painted with a number indicating the order in which it went in. After a while, the cousins jumped on the dollies and kicked off across the stage with a skateboarder's ease, and soon the boy-movers joined in. A clamor of roaring wheels and hollering boys filled the gym. Meanwhile, Owen charged around with manly vigor issuing directions. "Here, this one! Up! Got it! Let's move!" he told the boy-movers, pausing only to pat his face with the red bandana around his neck.

Dad changed into his street clothes behind his wardrobe trunk. The curtains were up by then, and all us girls saw his bony white legs in his plaid boxers. Crates moved down the ramp of the stage and up the ramp to the truck. Soon Dad jumped to help, in blue jeans, with a wide-brim Panama hat snug on his head.

The stage emptied and the truck filled. The boy-movers carried away the hobo luggage and wardrobe trunks on the dollies before rolling away the big gold hoop for The Floating Piano. Lastly, they dismantled the proscenium. The batons were lowered, black curtains untied, metal beams unhinged, floor panels unassembled and carried into the truck. Slowly, the magic show disappeared piece by piece. The clock on the gym wall read twenty minutes to midnight. We should have eaten and been traveling to our next town. Hospitalizations, sickness, injury, lawsuits…

What would happen now?

As Mom, Clair, and I gathered our things to leave, I felt good about our first show. We had subdued and entertained a big rowdy group. Before walking out, I turned around in the doorway to look at the gym. No sign of us remained. Considering the effort it took to get the show to Fairfield, I was shocked at how fast it was taken down.

That night we headed west and pulled into a motel with a vacancy sign. Because we were getting in late, Dad asked the hotel clerk for a late check-out, specifying that the maids were not to disturb us till then. He needed eight hours of sleep on the road to preserve his strength. Sleep. It was the fuel of a traveling showman.

In our room he took the phone off its hook, hung the Do Not Disturb sign on the door, and wedged the chair against it in case of robbers. From the suitcase he removed a leather pouch, telling Mom, "I got the G-U-N," which he kept by his side of the bed in case someone tried to break in. He changed into his green-striped pajamas and placed his yellow list on his bedside table. In the morning he would call the sponsors of the next show to confirm they had arranged for a local pianist for The Floating Piano. He also needed to know stage amenities. He needed the requisite spotlight and center steps down to the audience.

He walked to the bathroom, and I heard a clattering from Mom's makeup kit. Valium. Speed was one Rule of the Road, and sleep the other. He believed one night of little sleep could lead to another, creating a kind of snowball effect, wearing him down and risking his ability to perform. The pills were carefully broken into quarters and halves to keep his dosages exact. Too much and he lost his sharpness for the stage; too little and the road-hums wouldn't let him sleep.

We had two queen-size beds. Mom slept with me because Dad wanted the entire bed to ensure a sound sleep. I got under the covers and reached into my red tote bag to withdraw a tablet of paper. The *Reader's Digest* article.

How to begin? A journalist had to have a lead. I blinked at the empty page. So much had happened, I went blank. I was surprised by how stuck I was. It would have to please my father. I could feel him looking over my shoulder even before I wrote the first word. I thought about that noisy floating ball, which, of course, I could never write about. Finally, I put it away and pulled out my big red notebook, my journal. My hand swept across the page, all the excitement of the night tumbling out: the roving spotlight, dancing coins, cascading cards, Mom's robust bustling body, the hot sticky breath of the crowd, and the unearthly dance of The Floating Ball across the stage and its lonely whine on the wire. And there was more. As I wrote I kept sensing the greatest illusion would be the magic show itself, and I had to quickly record it as proof that it even happened.

12

JOURNEY TO GLORY WITH GEESE

At the end they hold out a big streamer with Grabel on it and i seack behind it from off stage and got on the peddleister where the hat is placed on and when they bring the hat down i squeeze through a flap and wait. And then i am produced. After that Mom does a lot. She comes out of boxes.

The Grabels, 1977

WE PLAYED IN ALL kinds of theaters. Cold and worn ones with rutted floors, and elegant ones with frilly curtains. We played junior college theaters, civic centers, and old downtown theaters that used to be vaudeville houses. Sometimes we didn't even have a stage, just a big, bleak room in a grange hall, armory, or fairgrounds. That was when we set up our proscenium, which we carried in the truck.
We girls dressed anywhere we could, in grimy bathrooms with bad lighting or in old chorus dressing rooms with sullied, paint-flecked

mirrors. Sometimes we dressed backstage behind drapes or foulards hung around our wardrobe cases.

Most often we played high school facilities, even though our show was not designed for kids. The local high school was often the only theatrical venue to which sponsors had access in town. Called a "multipurpose room," it was a gym with a stage facing center court. Chairs would be arranged in even rows across the court facing the stage.

These school stages were always deeply spare and modest, with lists of dos and don'ts on the wall for the students, and light-panel switches clearly labeled. A few times we played in posh new theaters filled with the scent of furniture polish and encore roses, and a sweeping expanse of red mohair seats, everything imbued with lofty Shakespearean aspirations. In those theaters, I always walked to the very top of the balcony seats to gaze down. Usually, curtains of heavy red velour flanked the stage. An expanse of burnished wood would run from the apron all the way upstage to the dark backdrop. I always got a little dizzy looking down into a stage's devouring mouth, with its red lusty lips and tawny tongue.

As soon as the show was over, we packed up the truck, moved to the next town, slept, unpacked at a new theater, and performed that night. Then the whole cycle started again. This is why a road man longs for a steady booking. He wants a dressing room where he can hang his clothes and keep tins of stage makeup on his vanity. He wants his magic cronies stopping by his little apartment near the theater to play poker after the show, to sleep in till dusk, and sip a bowl of soup before showtime. A road man can never have that. Time and motion commands his being, blood, and bones. By the time he drives out of town his audiences will be home in bed. He lives on in dim, frosty memory and the dreamscape of strangers.

During those early shows in San Rafael and Petaluma, I was in perpetual elation. Each time we rolled into town, I nearly expected champagne sent to our motel room and a reporter from the local newspaper waiting by the stage door. In my leap from the hat, I heard the hushed murmur of strangers—Brava, maestra, brava—imagined roses sent to my dressing room and well-wishers lining the road as we left town, my farewells called out from the speeding car window: au revoir, arrivederci, auf wiedersehen, my dear friends.

Then during The Opening in Fort Bragg, the geese defecated on the stage. Just as Brody picked up a goose after its appearance, it relieved itself. After all these years I can still see the disaster encapsulated in brilliant white light. The crowd jabbered. Little kids in the front yelled, "Gross!" A nightmare unfolded right before us and the music carried on. Dad produced the second goose. This one got Brody on the leg and continued as it was carried off. A Mississippi of waste zigzagged across the stage.

For a while we didn't know what to do. Clair, the boys, Owen, and I stood onstage with our faces twisted by indecision. Did we keep smiling, or did we join in the horror? Who knew? There wasn't even a Rule of the Road about it. Then the third goose nailed Dad in the leg.

That's when we let it go: "Ugh! Ewww!" we cried. "Ugh! Ewww!" the crowd cried. Now the stage floor was a slick hazard and everyone in tumult. I kept thinking Dad would stop the number, turn off the music, draw the drapes, get a mop, but he kept on, barreling through those droppings. I couldn't keep my head up, I was shrinking, drooping. My bedroom. If only I were there.

Continuing on with The Opening, Dad yanked foulards and bird cages from the top hat, minus his endearing winks and schmoozy smiles. When I jumped out of the hat, I landed lightly and ran off on tiptoes for fear I'd slip in the muck.

After the curtain closed, Dad stuck one leg through the curtain split, and Mom frantically cleaned his pant leg while he started the patter for The Coins. The theater manager brought us a mop and bucket, and we girls grabbed paper towels from the bathroom and started cleaning. I heard Dad begin the next act. "A silver disk, a silver dollar," he said, his patter sounding canned and flat. Halfway through, folks finally calmed down. A deep, sobering silence descended on them as they watched him traipse up and down the aisles, pulling coins from men's whiskers and behind lady's ears.

It was Ben's fault. We found him stage left wallowing in the shadows with his head in his hands. "I fed the geese before the show," he moaned. He didn't know the excitement of the stage and the food in their bellies would have such a disastrous consequence. Brody shoved his shoulder. "You dumbwit!"

The hardest part was continuing on with the show that night. My forced smile onstage quickly faded backstage. I hid in the dressing room a lot, refusing to acknowledge my invisible crowds in the mirror. I remember cleaning my shoes. My first high heels. It was heartbreaking to have walked through goose crap in them.

Backstage, I glared at Ben for being such a nincompoop, while inside my terror felt palpable. Dad had just told me casino talent scouts were attending our one show at the convention center in Las Vegas, and the possibility of such a mistake happening at that critical show was too awful to contemplate.

At intermission, Dad sat behind his wardrobe trunk, wiping off his patent leather shoes. I turned away, unable to erase the image of him maneuvering through the mess. Whatever horror I had suffered from those mocking girls felt negligible now. I sensed my father behind me, snapping on his sparkling sequin vest for the second half. He wasn't even going to cut the show short.

For the finale, we did The Cannon. As we stood in a row, bowing amid the glaring barrel and array of boxes, I noted the applause was firm and steady. The audience had moved on from the fiasco, and Dad had saved the show.

As I was winding up electrical cords, a little boy approached me. "Can I have your autograph?" He held out a pen and a show ticket. A tingle flew up my body, and I signed with a flourish. In that moment, I saw myself as he saw me—the girl in the top hat. I always landed on my high heels, neat like a pro.

"Las Vegas," I said out loud so my breath could give it life once more. In that deep, hushed sound, I discovered its promise, still fresh and unblemished.

13

PRACTICE IS NOT PERFECT

at dinner Dad got so excited when he told us about his new illusions. He had things flying over the audience heads People screaming and things falling down.

He says it would be the best show in Vegas, And i believe it would.

Helen from Oklahoma

IF THE MOST IMPORTANT Rule of the Road was speed, then Owen ranked supreme. Backstage and front stage, spinning and packing boxes, he exerted a frothy might that outshined Ben with his casual loping gait, and Brody who stopped work to skate around on the dolly. At first we were impressed by Owen's stamina, then we realized his quickness wasn't out of duty. His weedy body just couldn't be still. When our trio got to the high school multipurpose room in Yuba City, we paused long enough to watch Owen as he maneuvered a crate on a dolly by himself and rolled it down the ramp past the boy-movers.

We set up the show, Mom cuing the music at her table and me loading the top hat with its foam birds while the scent of hamburgers from the school cafeteria drifted around us. A girls' P.E. class played volleyball, and a cacophony of hollering and skidding sneakers reverberated throughout the gym. I observed Owen bounding around on his lanky legs, opening crates and rolling out equipment with his sinewy force. He then stopped and wiped his sweatless brow with his bandana. By that afternoon, when show duties were completed, Owen still had not sat down. He roamed the stage, passing by our trio with his fingers braided behind his neck to lock down his restless limbs.

Mom glanced with concern at our unanchored truck driver. "He's got ants in his pants," she said.

Dad arched an eyebrow. "More than just ants."

After the show that night, the curtain parted and in stepped Mazzie, his hair shellacked, wearing a moss-green leisure suit and stiff pointy Oxfords in horse brown. No one knew he was coming, and I felt flush with emotion to see someone from home. "Mazzie!" I exclaimed, hugging him and feeling his heavy, watery body in my thin arms.

"I came to see this swell show," he announced.

We gathered around him. "No autographs, please," he said, fussing with his jacket.

His nephews, Ben and Brody, offered him hardy handshakes.

"Tuck in your shirttail," he muttered to Brody, swatting his chest. "You're in the big time now. Your mother says you never call."

Brody pulled at a hank of his hair. "I *called* her."

Mom touched her powdery cheek against Mazzie's, reminiscent of those Magic Gal party greetings at our front door.

"You still got great gams, Helene," he said.

Dad stood behind his trunk, emptying his pockets, stashing items away in his top drawer. "How was The Pipe, Maze?"

"Cat's meow," he answered, drumming his fingers on his chest. Then he moved closer to Dad and reported in a low, raspy voice: "There's a big hullabaloo about your comeback, Lee. They even mentioned it on Johnny Carson. Ed McMahon said, 'I hear Grabel's back,' like it's the talk of the town."

At this exciting news, I gazed off dreamily and tried to imagine the name "Lee Grabel" uttered in the fabulous milieu of popular television.

"And someone overhead Blackstone Jr. talking in an elevator in

Hollywood," he panted. "He's beefing up his show with you around."

After the grievous warnings from the Magic Gal magicians, I was relieved Mazzie had good news for us. Dad played it cool, barely nodding his head.

We went back to Mazzie's hotel room after the show. From his suitcase he removed a long metal tube with a leather strap.

"What's that?" the cousins asked. They had never seen that tube, not once in the shows that Mazzie had performed for their birthday parties as kids.

He pulled out a long, black, white-tipped cane from the case. A loop of upholstery string dangled from its top. He slipped his ring finger into the loop, and the cane turned upright in the air and just hung there. A deep silence descended on us. We couldn't turn away. Mazzie moved back, and the cane moved forward. Mazzie moved left, the cane moved right. He bounced around to and fro while the fitful cane swayed, bobbed, and spun in a circle just beyond his thick fingers. When I turned my eyes fuzzy wuzzy, the string disappeared, and I saw something truly magical, Mazzie dancing with a floating cane.

Owen slapped his knee. "You magicians!"

Mazzie and the cane mingled, not unlike two woozy people at a cocktail party. From my seat in the corner, I flashed back to Mom's parties where Mazzie had huffed, mumbled, and lumbered about with all the other curmudgeonly magicians. Now I could see a glimmer of the performer he once was.

"Let me see that," Dad said. He wrapped the loop around his finger and did the same dance, and I wondered if they'd both attended the same dancing-cane class. Dad and the bouncing cane orbited around each other until I was unsure which one moved the other.

Brody's face was jabbed with light.

"How'd you guys do that?" he asked in a hot rush.

Mazzie lowered himself onto the bed with his hands as though his back hurt. "Didn't eat, didn't sleep, didn't go anywhere. All I did was practice that thing."

Dad dropped the cane back in its tube. "Nothing happens unless you make it happen," he said firmly.

Folks were always so wrong about magic. It wasn't easy or natural. To suspend a disco globe between two pale, fallow palms required all kinds of tools. And if that wasn't magic, then what was? I looked across the room. Not everyone understood magic's travails. Brody had watched the cane dance with the flicker of big ideas on his saucy face. Now, he looked at the tube which housed the cane, and declared, "Pretty cool." Then he imitated the sway of the cane dance with the lightness of a football player dodging tackles on his way to a touchdown.

The next day, as I loaded the cages of fake birds into the big hat backstage, Brody walked up to Dad with his fists jammed in his pockets. "Could you teach me a trick? Just somethin'?"

We were playing a sterile, airless room in a glassy new civic center. My nose tingled from the scent of carpet cleaner. Through the curtain, I heard a loud banging and clashing as men arranged rows and rows of metal chairs for the night's show.

Dad tilted his head thoughtfully. "Cards are a good starter," he suggested, and opened the top drawer of his wardrobe trunk. He removed a jack of spades from a speckled Bee deck and traveled it around his hand, crushing it in his palm and gripping it between his fingers. Seeing Brody's earnest focus, Dad slowed it down. "Now watch," he instructed. He broke it down to a few gradual moves: a clutch, a slide, bend into the palm, a flick. The jack appeared and vanished, rose and fell, in a careful duet with his hand.

From behind a cage with a scraggy foam macaw, I watched Brody give it a try, positioning and repositioning his jellyfish fingers. It was the classic back and front palm, a beginner's step for every aspiring card king. As hard as Brody concentrated, it was a fragile setup in his awkward hands. Those cards subdued him, commanded him, and stole the twitchy wisecracks right out of his mouth. A card fluttered to the floor.

"Your fingers are longer," Brody reasoned.

Dad spread them out. "They're just strong," he replied. It was true. No one needed long fingers to be a magician, only strong ones and desire to match. He gave Brody a little group of his cards and said, "Remember, for every move onstage there's a hundred hours of practice."

We'd been on the road a week when Brody started practicing cards. While Ben kept a bag of soup crackers in his shirt pocket to feed wild birds, Brody stashed cards in his, their blood-red and ebony edge brimming the top. He palmed them before and after the show, backstage between acts, and below the table at restaurants. Over the next few days, Dad had lots of advice. "Poker-size cards and bridge cards will hurt the reputation of a card-man. Keep your hands clean, soft, and warm. For flourish work, Blue Ribbon is best."

I suspect my father was less committed to turning Brody into a magician than into a good assistant. Under his tutelage, he might groom the young man into trusted right-hand help. By then it was clear Owen was too erratic and Ben too lackadaisical, and Brody was smart if a bit scattered. Before each show, I watched him walk around with his bow tie dangling from his fingers looking for someone to tie it. I loved the soft spot above his lip, the gentle swirl of his hair with its strands of dirty red.

I could only hope the forces of the magic show might bring us together.

A few days later, on a small, unswept stage outside of Vacaville, I saw that gentle swaying dance I knew so well. Dad was teaching Brody his One-Handed Card Production. Side by side, Brody mimicked him in the push and pull of the cards. Dad's original move. It had to mean something. My father's trust. Brody's eagerness. I felt possibility stirring. Maybe Brody would meld into our trio and inhabit our big dream with us. I imagined him escorting me to swanky high-roller restaurants or telling me jokes in a red-cushioned dressing room, both of us onstage circling my father in hazy fallen light. I paused in the doorway unable to move, so overcome by what it meant.

"Do it this way," Dad instructed, as Brody arranged his fingers and lowered his gaze.

At the threshold of my father's world, his glib commentary was replaced with sweet sincerity.

To slip into the crux of Brody's shoulder and feel his arms around me was perhaps the most wonderful of all my wishes and crazed fantasies. Just the prospect of it stopped my heart and feet from moving. I passed their huddled figures, my head down, shy from my thoughts. Except for a few little kisses in grade school, I was chaste. The new frontier of boys scared me, and I was good at averting my eyes around them. I had completely absorbed my mother's unspoken expectations about boys and dating. I didn't dare want more than a kiss or a hug. Still, his presence opened up warm, smoky places I had never been before.

That night as I pulled up my black leotard and slipped on my rhinestone-edged vest, I wondered how my sexiness measured up. I had long legs and a burgeoning bosom. I hoped to turn his head; even a flirty eye slanted my way would be encouraging. Instead, I saw only cool indifference as he swept by me backstage. Sitting down, I poked around my cosmetic bag and thought about The Backstage. There was a moment during the trick when we were close. When I entered the door into the box, Brody was only a foot away. He always took off his shoes so he could move around the box unhampered, and I would sense him near me, crouching in the dark in his stocking feet. I'd hear the illusion's tinny music through the box, and the soft rustle of his polyester pants. Then I'd slide the trap door open and slip down into the bottom compartment.

Sharing that dark, secret space with Brody thrilled me, and that night our moment in the box felt special to me. *He must feel it, too.* We were alone, beyond the spotlight or crowd or crew. *Speak to me.* I tried to will his playful words, anything. Sinking into the trap, I curled my spine and tucked my knees against my chest. There was a soft thump overhead as Brody closed the lid over me. It sounded decisive: *thud, bam, be gone.* A clear rebuff to my hopes. It was so disappointing. His "Brace Face" teasing had ceased, and I didn't know why.

It wasn't that different with the rest of the crew. I still found myself an outsider to their friendly gabbing. In the afternoon, I would see them by the truck talking while Ben tended to the animals. Or sometimes if we played a theater in town, they would take off for lunch, heads thrown back, smiles open to the sky, Owen leading the way with his big, willful stride. I would think of them sharing French fries at some nearby hamburger joint while I ate a deli sandwich backstage with my parents in a dark so quiet I felt trapped in perpetual preshow dusk. I always listened for the crew's return.

First, their footsteps shattering the thick quiet, and then their jabbering. "I can't help it if you're a stupid ass…You started it… You didn't even use it right…It's busted, I tell you." Clair often came across as a wiser cohort. "You should try reading the directions when all else fails."

I didn't know how to join their clowning. To compensate, I continued to repeat remarks I'd heard from my parents. "Lincoln Continentals have plenty of leg room" or "That Bobby Darin sure gave Sinatra a run for his money." My precociousness might have been endearing, but I was precocious in the wrong ways. Only people over fifty liked me.

Sometimes Clair would put down her book and point her pert librarian nose at me. "You need help with schoolwork?"

I always said no. Being her dutiful student wasn't the relationship I had signed up for. On the road it was easy to forget about school until we passed a yellow bus or loitering truants in front of a convenience store.

One night it occurred to me I might never be included in the crew's outings. We'd been on the road ten days by then and were settling into our relationships with each other. I was standing at the stage door watching folks park and leave their cars with tickets in their hands. I felt a little lonely thinking about the weeks ahead on my own. That night, as we waited behind the curtain for the show to start, exchanging nervous smiles, I felt deep affection for our four helpers. If I wasn't their chum, then I was a beloved cheery mascot of the magic show. How fortunate they were to even be here. Dad and I were rescuing Owen, Clair, and the boys from tiny, inaudible lives, and we had to include them in our big casino booking.

Meanwhile, the towns flew by. Oroville, Willow, Red Bluff... Concerns about Owen continued. After one show Dad put his hand on Owen's shoulder and advised him about "pacing," as we had three more months to go. Dad feared Owen might burn out. Their chat only charged him up, and the next night we watched his face redden as he wrapped his long arms around the piano crate and lifted three corners off the stage. After the show that night, we girls sat on gym bleacher seats watching Owen outwork the young boy-movers, stopping only to pat his dry face with the red bandana.

That night in the car Dad predicted, "He's bound to crash."

The truck carried all the show equipment, including the animals. Our trailer was forty feet long, with a stall for Frankie, and the tractor had a shiny silver step up into the cab. It was completely white, as white as the white-hot center of a spotlight. We didn't use Frankie in many shows, because most venues were not suited for a horse. Only stages with a flat, wide passageway from the truck to the stage would do. When we did play such a venue, Frankie was never onstage for long. As soon as we enclosed her in the four panel walls, Ben would unzip a flap of fabric for Frankie's exit. The panels were positioned upstage against the backdrop to prevent the audience from seeing her leave. Backstage, Mom parted the backdrop, and Frankie and Ben would walk straight out. Frankie was usually back in her stall by the time the trick ended. Certainly, a traveling road show did not provide ideal conditions for a horse. On days off, we tried to park the truck near a grazing field, and we made sure she had all the hay and oats she wanted.

During our day off in Chico, we parked the truck in a weedy lot down the road from our motel. That morning Dad and I stopped by. Frankie was tied to the truck bumper eating a pile of hay. When we got out of the car, she turned to watch us. Just below her large, fathomless eyes, a white blaze in the shape of a diamond covered the bridge of her nose. The geese waddled around the truck, cronking and pecking at the grass. On the truck hood was our cage of six white Java doves. A little farm scene played out right next to the freeway. Ben threw down hay and geese feed and lugged in water from a nearby irrigation system. From the car window, I noted his skill and comfort with his duties. I could almost believe he'd grown up on a farm, which I knew wasn't the case. I suspect he enjoyed caring for our critters in the morning sunshine more than he did the artificial drama of the magic show.

When Brody saw us there, he jumped down from the sleeper cab and stretched his arms overhead in a bearish yawn. Dad offered to bring them food for dinner, only to have the cousins point at a pizza parlor down the road and say they'd go there. Owen was in a nearby motel, and Clair was in another motel across town.

A couple drove by the truck, their mouths agape. We were a curious outfit with the fowl and grazing horse. I watched the couple as they turned, craning their necks to stare. The truck was devoid of advertisements, as Dad wanted to protect it from the usual mischievous delinquents.

"Remember," he said, glaring warily at the departing car. "Just tell folks it's a private job. You're moving a rancher across country."

As we drove away, I glanced back at the truck with its long trailer, a snow-capped mountain range in the distance.

Early the next morning the phone rang in our motel.

Dad answered it. "Yes...I see...Is everyone okay?"

I rubbed my eyes and peeped out from under the covers. Dad's hair was sticking up from sleep, refashioning him into a bedraggled wizard. Mom stirred.

He hung up the phone and grabbed his pants. "They crashed the truck last night," he reported.

Mom swung her legs out of the bed. "What?"

He zipped up his ankle boots, his movements fast and voice calm. "They hit a man's car. That's who called."

Mom touched her chest in shock. "How bad is it?"

A mangled bumper. It had been parked on the street when the truck hit it. He needed to give the man a check for damages. "Brody gave him our number at the motel."

He was leaving now to see the crew. We would stay another night in Chico and then drive to our show in Susanville the next day. He stuck the Panama hat on his head and muttered, "Strength give me," and left.

Mom and I waited for hours at the motel room, unable to focus on our books and magazines. I kept thinking of Dad's words: *They crashed the truck.* My head spun. In a few hours he returned with the crew's story. Clair had wanted to move to a cheaper motel, so Owen and the boys unhitched the tractor from the trailer. With all four crammed in the front of the truck, they goofed around. Owen got distracted and hit the parked car.

"Why didn't they call us last night?" Mom asked.

"They said they didn't want to worry us."

"That's hogwash," she said.

"Well, that's what they said," he replied shortly.

I sat quietly on the bed, numbly staring at the bedspread's cheerless angular pattern. It was hard to say what was worse, the crew's misdeeds or Brody's disloyalty. I glanced at Dad, who was dialing his insurance agent. We both had hoped Brody would be good help in the magic show. Now I didn't know. And Owen's behavior had been so strange lately.

"Do you think Owen's on drugs?" Mom asked with quiet concern.

Dad contemplated the carpeted floor. "Maybe."

The next night at the Redding show, as we waited onstage for the curtain to open, I glanced behind me. Owen stared straight-faced at the curtain. He had splashed himself with water and his cheeks were red, his hair colorless and slick. One bloodshot eye twitched. Next to him, Brody admired his cuff links. When the curtain opened, I dragged up a smile.

After the show, we went to a local diner for a late-night breakfast. One big table wasn't available, so we split up into two tables, my parents and I in one, the crew in the other. Our trio glumly ate our eggs while the crew laughed with hooligan glee in the booth next to us. I heard Brody's smart remarks copied from Steve Martin monologues. "Well, excuuuuuse me!"

A part of me wanted to join their rebel laughter. Another part of me felt the icy knife of betrayal. Liars. Outlaws. They'd unhitched the tractor knowing Dad would never approve. Recklessly drove around town. Beer. I'm sure beer had something to do with it. I tried to ignore their laughter even as it roared through my head, twisting into a cyclone of hurt.

Meanwhile, my parents shot coded glances at our troublesome crew over their cups of coffee. They had differing views of the situation than I did. When they were younger, their crew had been their peers. This time, the age differences complicated the relationship. My parents were no longer young renegades, and more was at stake.

That night in the motel room, I sat down on the bed. The crew's actions smacked of rejection of our trio and the show. Katy Gwabel flared up, sad and fluid. My sobs were sudden and intense. "They hate me!"

Mom was fast with her kindly assurances. "They like you! Of

course they do!" Tears streamed down my face while she fetched tissue. She handed a wad to me. "You're perfect the way you are." It was one of those dumb things parents said when they didn't understand.

I heard Dad's voice. "Helene, take care of it." I lifted my head. He was pointing at me with anger, and I didn't know why. Then he sat down in the chair, flopped open a newspaper, and started to read. He was going to ignore my anguish. My heart plummeted. Hadn't I been his biggest ally in this dream, more than Mom? It made me cry harder, the tears flowing fast as he turned the pages and scanned the headlines. For the first time, my cherished show duties felt hollow. I had become static and shadow again.

Strong emotion made my father uncomfortable. And he probably feared I would hold grudges against my crewmates and violate one of the Rules of the Road—*don't let personal grievances get in the way of your show duties*. On some level, I must have questioned my value to him. I had slipped into my father's magic show effortlessly, blended into it like black thread against a Mylar curtain. Even then, with the tears flowing down my face, I would not have believed there could be a price to pay. For both of us.

The next day, our trio stopped by the truck on the way to breakfast. We had to drive to Susanville for our show tomorrow. Owen sat on the ground, leaning against the truck tire, staring blankly into space. I'd never seen him this still. He wasn't even wearing his red bandana.

Dad greeted him. Silence.

"What happened?" Dad asked the cousins.

"He's been that way all morning," Brody said, breaking Dad's gaze.

Dread squeezed the air out of me. Something was wrong with Owen. We needed him to drive the truck and tend the piano. Without him we'd have to end the tour. I thought of our trek back to Alamo, southward, me curled up in the backseat, everything gone to black.

I followed Dad back to the Cadillac. He was going to tell Mom we had to go home. He stopped at the passenger seat window, and Mom deeply inhaled and looked up at him, expecting the worst. "What's happening now?"

He passed the back of his hand across his mouth. "Now he's on downers," he said, wearily. "I'll call Al."

Al Lewis arrived that night. He and Dad gave Owen money and sent him home on a bus.

14

GUYS, HOLD THE SAUCE

I'am crumbled up in this tiny bathroom, my feet against the bath tub and my back aganist the wall. I can feel my tummy rolls under my gown in this position. I just couldn't fall asleep and i, all of a sudden began thinking up all thease things i wanted to say

The Great Alexander and Lee

AL JOINED OUR SHOW, arriving in his black sedan, with a tool kit, shoe polish, his wife, Dot, and an iron for his ruffled shirts. He could break down the piano lickety-split and park the big truck blindfolded. He liked a good game of blackjack and, if feeling festive, a martini, chilled and shaken, with a dash of olive brine and sweet vermouth. And after one or two, he could recite all thirty-eight presidents and forty-two vice presidents in chronological order forward and backward. He knew jugglers and clowns and loaned money to old down-and-out vaudeville men.

At our after-show meals, he was our court jester. Most of the time we couldn't stop laughing. Grabbing his water glass, he would give it a drunkard's wobbly swirl. "Some weasel took the cork out of my lunch." And we would laugh hard with mouths open, weak with silliness and gasping for air. These meals were a melee of old jokes and table gags, bent spoons and pennies in sugar packs, or Al impersonating a blue blood who drank coffee with his pinky up. Al's jokes were so old they were new. "What's on your tie? Oh, I thought it was your lunch!" he'd say, tapping his glass and saucer with his knife, mimicking that old cymbal and foot drum gag at the end of punchlines.

Dad often joined the hoopla by making his paper napkin dance. He'd pull up a corner so that it stood upright in his hands, and then he'd make it sway and bob by invisible strings.

Al kept him in line. "Oh, stop it, Lee. You're making the joint look shabby!" Or sometimes Dad would just plead with us. "Please! Don't stand in front of the cannon when it goes off. People might think it's not real!" We laughed loud and hard, unable to breathe, like we didn't care if laughter killed us.

Then one night something happened. In a Eureka diner, sitting around a big corner booth, I looked at their seven smiling faces and realized we had changed. No longer were we strangers to each other. We were a crew of a magic show. We were the Pocus Posse. The Great Grabel was the king of our crew. Helene, our veteran box jumper. Clair, the only showgirl to carry rulers and yellow No. 2 pencils. The boys, our trusty muscle pushing four tons of equipment. Dot, our cotton candy vendor. And Al, also known as The Great Alexander, slaying us nightly with his one-liners. "I would rather starve than do anything but magic, and now I do both."

From my purse I removed my small purple notebook. I was so enthralled by the Pocus Posse, I recorded our chatter. A lot of it was definitions of showbiz lingo. SRO: standing room only. Shill: person in show, impersonating an audience member. Prestidigitator: a magician. Bubbles: name for showgirls. Giggle water: alcohol. Bourbalina: nickname of a former assistant who drank lots of bourbon. Most of the notebook was filled with Dad's and Al's old jokes.

As I jotted, Dad threw back his shoulders and gave me a pleased sidelong glance. He thought I was taking notes for the *Reader's Digest* article. I turned away. I still hadn't written a word.

"Stick with me, kid," he teased, "and you'll be wearing potatoes as big as diamonds."

"Watch it, Lee. Or she'll want a star on her door," Al said, giving me an exaggerated wink.

Dad took out his wallet and flipped it open to a photo. "Who's that girl?" She had long brown hair and a big buck-toothed smile. My fourth-grade photo, the grade of my most incriminating act.

"My best card trick! You told them!" His big smile could not conceal the shadow that fell across his face. I had committed a serious offense.

"It was for *show* and *tell,* Dad," I said, with plenty of sass.

Dot leaned across the table. "All magicians are kooks, Kate." Al's wife was a short, fiery woman who always carried a lit cigarette between two straight fingers. She told me that when she married Al he was a bartender, and then one morning he pulled a red silk out of an egg. He had never told her he was a magician. The magic gatherings she attended quickly bored her. "Magicians can talk for hours about some little pocket trick," she said, fiercely rubbing her fingers together. "I won't pick a card anymore. I just refuse!"

Suddenly, a pall fell over the table. Dad leaned forward and craftily turned left and right in case the place was bugged. "Hank the Magician could be playing Klamath Falls," he told us in a near whisper.

Another magician was on our route.

"He's burning territory," Dad said grimly.

I turned to Mom for an explanation. She said when a bad show plays a town it hurts business for the next show coming through. *Burning territory.* I wrote it in my purple notebook with a lengthy definition, all caps.

"Or he might play after us in Corvallis," he worried.

This was also bad news. Sometimes a bad show intentionally played after a good show because the crowds are more likely to buy a ticket.

"Let's hope he heads north to Canada. Or it's curtains for us," Dad warned.

Al stirred cream into his coffee and said, "Maybe your bad jokes will kill him."

Al told all kinds of jokes. Corny jokes, stolen jokes, forgotten jokes, old jokes. He even had dirty jokes and once he told me one. We were crossing a street to a restaurant and when he came to the punch line, I laughed without even understanding it. The next day backstage when no one was around, he apologized to me. "I shouldn't have done that. I'm sorry."

Inside his wallet, he carried a professional studio shot of him when he was a young, wishful Hollywood actor. He stood in front of a white pillar in a silky tuxedo with his thick jet-black hair gelled into an elegant swirl around his head. A cigarette dangled from his fingers. He might have been a wealthy buckaroo, a sexy worldly man. His resemblance to old-time actor Clark Gable was uncanny. He impersonated the actor's most famous movie line, "Frankly my dear, I don't give a damn."

I didn't know much about Al except that he helped my parents in their show. Adults with exciting pasts were common to me. I believed Al had more funny stories to tell. That night I asked him, "What other magicians have you helped?"

He pondered his empty yolk-smeared plate. "Nobody." My good humor plummeted. I had insulted him somehow. I didn't understand back then that Al's magic expertise and drunk imitations were from his popular magic act he had performed around the country, including at the Magic Castle in Hollywood. The Great Alexander wasn't just his nickname. It was his professional stage name. He had taught at Chavez School of Magic in Los Angeles and helped many magicians develop their routines. He was a talented magician, a professional dancer, and a natural teacher in that he was knowledgeable and patient. I don't know why he worked with my parents for so many years as background help. Beneath all that jesting was a kind, gentle spirit that had been a mismatch for the harshness of showbiz. Maybe he'd found a safe haven in the company of my parents and their magic show.

After our meal, we walked outside into drifts of fog that coiled around us, stinging our faces and curling our hair. A lone white seagull squawked overhead as we scurried to our vehicles. Dad, Mom, Clair, and I to the Cadillac, the boys and Al to the big white truck, and Dot to her and Al's shiny sedan. I watched Al climb into the cab with his white socks flashing below his trouser hem. I didn't know how to make things right with him.

Al still remembered the peculiarities of the magic show. The hidden doors that creaked and the rough edges that could snag a silk. Standing backstage, he could feel the show's heartbeat and know if something was amiss. He handled the show's most sensitive tasks with competence and skill. He fired pellets of black powder into a cap from a sawed-off rifle for that *Boom!* in The Cannon. He did a splashy costume change with Dad in The Cut-Up Illusion, and he was responsible for all backstage duties with the piano, including strapping the player into the chair.

He was also pivotal in assisting Mom in her most crucial feat of box jumping, that deranged, unregal scramble backstage from the cannon base to the table trap for The Cannon. With her legs still in the cannon base, she would wrap her arms around Al's neck, and he would forcefully pull himself backward to pull her out. Then he would pick her up and set her down in the table trap as smooth as moving a hot dog to a different bun. And if this wasn't enough, Al understood the fundamentals of a good magic show and the nuance of artifice. Sophisticated hokum was his specialty, as was evident in The Escape Box.

The Escape Box was actually a publicity gimmick used to arouse interest and sell tickets. It had Houdini-style drama with a touch of graceless spectacle that Dad wasn't shy about. The sponsors of a town would arrange for him to escape from a box built by their local lumberyard, and a few days before the show, the town's newspaper would run a photo of the box, the headlines reading something like "Jack's Lumber Builds Box for Magician's Escape Next Tuesday." Dad and Al had to bluff their way through it, Dad pretending it was a fortified magician-proof box and Al feigning panic when the time was right.

Onstage, Dad would interrogate the lumberyard men, pointing his finger at them and bellowing his questions with lots of dramatic swagger.

"Did you gentlemen build this box?"

"We did, sir."

"Is it a strong, solid box, men?"

"Yes, sir."

"Do you think a man nailed inside that box could escape?"

"No, sir."

"We'll see about that!" he would say, winking at the crowd to assure them he wasn't one of those men. He then told them to count the minutes and gave instructions: "My assistants have been instructed to call an ambulance if I am not out in four minutes."

The box would be constructed of pallet boards, about thirty inches long by twenty inches wide by twenty-four inches high with an unhinged lid. Dad would step in the box, and then into a big red bag. One of the lumberyard men would tie his wrists together, and Dad would sink down into the bag, and they'd tie the bag at the top. Then they would nail down the lid with Dad inside. I carried out a big red tent, and everyone pulled on a corner of it, and the tent would lift off the ground and form around the box. We would then wait in cathedral silence with the audience.

After a minute or so, Al would come onstage, look at the closed tent and exit. In a bit he reappeared, this time glancing at his watch, visibly anxious. The third time he would rush onstage clutching a hatchet, as if this night, of all nights, a serious mishap had occurred. The crowd murmured. The magician was suffocating to death! Al would lunge for the box, hatchet in hand, ready to break it apart. That's when a voice called out from the back of the auditorium. "Are you expecting someone?" All heads would turn. Dad stood there with his arms crossed, beaming his faultless orthodontic smile. As he trotted down the aisle, with an arm raised in triumph, no one noticed Al silently strolling offstage, hatchet in hand.

Once Al joined the show, I hardly ever thought of Owen, and if I did, I imagined him on a southbound bus, red bandana around his neck as he finally succumbed to sleep. I didn't know how much we needed Al until he joined us. The show felt less wobbly, less a finicky old house with careless occupants and bad plumbing. All its parts started to work together, and with the smooth execution of the big illusions, we started to trust the show's ability to entertain.

At her backstage table, Mom would whisper to me, "I'm so glad Al's here." Glancing into the stage-left shadows, I would imagine him standing alert in his pointy bow tie listening for the show's whimpers and missed beats, with an attaché case full of solutions at his feet.

Soon we were left with only one thing to do—surrender to the road. Except not everything was right. Ben and Brody couldn't get the show packed up in time. Often when the boy-movers arrived at the end of the show, the crates were still unpacked and everyone had to wait. Sometimes the entire load-out took more than two hours, with we girls stiff in our seats waiting and the boy-movers up past their bedtimes on a school night. Dad told the cousins again and again, "Pack as you go." As soon as a routine ended, equipment was to be rolled back into its case and latched shut, ready for the truck. Nevertheless, night after night, the cousins packed at the end of the show.

By the time we hit the Oregon border, we'd been on the road seventeen days, and we were still late getting out. I sat on the bald mohair seat of a dreary old downtown theater and watched another group of boy-movers with their hands jammed in the pockets of their varsity jackets huddled next to closed curtains. If the local high school football team was not put to work soon, they might bail on us for someone's rec room.

In the front row, Lions Club members settled finances with Dad, who had dressed down to his stiff white shirt, black pants, and shiny patent-leather shoes. His face gleamed from his bronze makeup, and he could have passed for a displaced aristocrat. On his lap was an open manila folder filled with ticket receipts and the contract for that night's show. Every now and then he glanced fretfully at the boy-movers. If they abandoned us, we would have to pack the truck ourselves.

Dot appeared with her purse tucked under her arm, her small, imposing figure as sturdy and solid as forged iron. Some nights she set up a cotton candy and ice cone concession stand. At the end of each night, I always asked her how it went. On low-sale nights, Dot would scowl at me, insulted I had asked. On good nights the cash in her wallet elated her.

"Kate," she'd say, rockets in her eyes. "I made some *good money.*"

Tonight was a rocket night. "There were so many people, the janitor's wife had to help," she gushed. "I gave her twenty bucks, right off the top!"

She sat down next to me and happily bounced her purse on her knee. I studied her small feet in her small black high heels, cute enough for a doll.

Mom and I were unsure if Dot liked us. Maybe she thought we were snobs because we lived in a nice house. Dot used to waitress at a famous restaurant on Sunset Boulevard, and she enjoyed telling us stories about the celebrities she'd served. When she discovered Mom and I had never eaten at or heard of the famous restaurant on Sunset Boulevard, she blinked at us, speechless. Maybe she considered us worse than snobs and worse than magicians.

After a few drinks she would call Dad "Mr. Wonderful." She knew we needed Al's help, and she would often say, "Where would you be without us?"

I was a little afraid of her. Dot did not make a fuss over me the way other adults did. She glowered at my most innocuous remarks. *What's your favorite color? The bathroom's out of toilet paper! I'll have the low-cal plate…with a milkshake.* Some middle grade-schoolers were taller than Dot, and it's possible her disparaging glares ensured folks would take her seriously and never call her cute or cuddly or say her shoes belonged to a doll.

As she flipped the switch of her lighter, a blue flame caught the tip of her cigarette. She saw me watching her and held it out to me. "You want a drag?" A naughty shine flickered in her stormy dark eyes. She saw me as the young woman I was becoming way before I did. Sometimes she nudged me along.

I declined her offer even as I imagined that long white cigarette on my lips.

When Mom joined us, Dot quizzed her on cooking. "Oh, Helene, you don't flambé?" Fried chicken was a hot topic. Dot soaked her chicken in buttermilk for twelve hours and was horrified to learn

Mom only tossed hers around in cream. She straightened her spine and said, "It couldn't be very juicy then."

Mom's shrug showed great modesty, considering her famed fried chicken had been proclaimed by legions to be the best on this continent and beyond. "Folks don't complain," was all she said. Then, moving her leg, Mom accidentally dumped her purse. Lipstick capsules, coin pouch, powder compacts, white handkerchief, pens, and paper receipts covered the yucky floor. To see us foraging for stray items amid all her concession trash delighted Dot. "You two look like complete dopes!"

That's when Dot started warming up to us, even to Mom's chicken. "I bet it's tender and crispy," she remarked soon after. When she noticed me wearing lipstick, she said, "You're a real showgirl now, aren't you Kate?" She had a deep, rolling laugh for such a small person, and her artless gruff didn't feel so threatening once in her favor.

When the curtains opened, crates were latched and a cool breeze blew in through the open doors of the loading dock, chilling our arms and faces. The cousins and the boy-movers started pushing crates. The stage slowly emptied. Box numbers 1, 2, 3, 4…into the truck. Dad jumped in, pushing crates and directing boy-movers. After midnight, the truck was loaded.

On my way to the Cadillac with my red tote bag I passed Dad, who was reminding the cousins of the Rules of the Road.

"Pack as you go," he urged them. "That's how we did it every night with the old show."

"It's a lot of stuff," Ben muttered.

"That's impossible," Brody added.

When Dad got into the car, he sounded annoyed. "Impossible, my foot."

Mom rubbed her neck. "What are they doing backstage the whole night?" she asked.

"They say they're busy." He turned on the engine and drove out of the lot. "I don't know what they're doing."

I was tired of waiting for them, too. Over the last few weeks, cold and hungry for dinner, I had sat in many bleachers or on hard metal chairs looking at a closed curtain while the boys finished up. If they were not packing up during the show, then what were they doing? Deep inside, I knew. They were telling jokes, leaning on crates, thinking about waffles after the show. My heart collapsed a little. How could they?

Hours later, in the stiffly starched sheets of our darkened motel room, I was still hurt. I heard my father's unsteady breathing. Maybe he was awake too, thinking about our boys, picturing their sagging, smirking figures in the backstage light. I thought of them right then, tucked into their bedrolls in the truck's sleeper cab surrounded by their duffel bags of dirty laundry, snoozing away.

On our day off in Coos Bay, Dad complained about the boys to Al in our motel room. "You might as well take over the loading out. The boys can't do it," he said, clearly frustrated.

"They're not even amateurs, Lee," Al replied darkly. "They're kids."

On the way out the door, Al did a Groucho Marx impersonation for me, tapping an air cigar at his mouth and saying, "Hey Kate, I could dance with you until the cows come home. On second thought, why don't I dance with the cows till you come home!" My offending little remark had been forgotten, and I was relieved he hadn't taken it seriously.

The next night at a junior college in Roseburg, Al had the curtain up in less than ten minutes after the show. The boy-movers swarmed the stage, and crates moved. When they were done, Dad laid his hand on Brody's back and showed him his wristwatch. It read 10:45 p.m.

"Impossible, you say?" he said and walked away with enough bounce to suggest Brody was full of malarkey. Brody thrust out his jaw, thunderheads rising in his gunmetal eyes. He grunted and snapped the dolly up with his foot and caught it. He was still stubborn to be right. "This show isn't so hot," he grumbled.

I winced, stung by his remark, and gazed down at the tatty pine stage floor.

Suddenly, Dot was there, shaking a finger and leveling him with one of her scowls. "Don't knock success, kid." She had become the new defender of our show. Brody walked away in response to this playground of bullies.

"You wanna go with me?" Dot called after him. He hated riding with Al and Ben in the truck as it had no backseat and they made him sit between them up front.

Watching them walk outside toward the sedan, I thought of Dot's steely glares and knew Brody would never get by unscathed. As they drove out of the lot, I caught a glimpse of Dot through the car window, sitting close to the steering wheel so her short arms could reach it, talking and waving her cigarette around. Brody was slumped down, probably finding refuge in the cards flicking through his fingers.

After that, Dad and Brody's little card lessons ceased, and there were other changes as well. Not only did his "Brace Face" teasing stop, he outright ignored me. To love is to live in the drama of absence. He never spoke to me. What hurt most was his pretty-boy profile always turned away from me. Maybe my little-sister status had worn thin, or maybe I got tangled up in his relationship with my father. Soon his indifference became so palpable I could touch and carry it with me. I resigned myself to being a shy admirer as he strode by in his ruffled blue shirt, a bridegroom fleeing a wedding.

When we did The Backstage, I filled the space we shared with questions: *Why don't you see me? Why don't you care?* At our diner meals, I hoped his gaze would pause on me, just for a moment, to make me feel visible.

Two days later, we played an old grange hall at the bottom of the Cascade mountain range. It was cold, and someone turned on the gas heater, which clanked and moaned as we set up the show. Through swinging double doors, I found a kitchen with a big black eight-burner gas stove caked with crud. A nice man swept the old plank floor and told Dad they had no follow spotlight.

"All right, thank you," Dad said politely, no doubt disappointed. Meager strip lighting never did the show justice.

We played for about sixty people that night, a fine show, except each time we opened and closed the drape it kicked up dust. Then, during Dad's card routine, we lost sound. The music stopped and Dad's microphone died. Mom quickly checked the tape recorder. The "play" button was pushed, the tape turning, and the equipment plugged in.

"Heavens to Betsy!" she exclaimed, clutching air with her empty hands. We fluttered around the table in a panic. I beckoned to Brody walking by.

"Do something!" Mom cried. "We have no sound!"

He studied the huge tangle of cords behind the table.

Onstage, Dad projected his voice out to the crowd. "Watch closer, ma'am. Fingers open, right over here, a card. And oh, look, here's another one, right to my fingers." Without the music his patter didn't sound very amusing. I could hear his cards creaking through his fingers and his shoes clapping across the stage.

Looking up, I saw the back of Brody's head, his auburn locks tickling his neck, as he walked away.

Mom lurched forward as if to pull him back. "Where are you going?" she called out in dismay. "This is an emergency!"

He shrugged. "I don't know what's wrong with it," he said and kept on.

I watched after him, eyes wide with disbelief. Mom grabbed her head and let go a guttural "Uhhhhhhh!" Onstage, Dad's voice strained to reach the back seats.

Suddenly, Al appeared with a grange hall man who opened the electric panel.

Dad's routine was winding down, and still the speakers issued no sound. The Vanishing Horse was next. Clair and I carried our panel into the wings and waited. Ben walked by in his loping stride.

Mom ran up to him. "Where's the horse?"

His brown eyes flew open. "Helene," he said, dumbfounded. "There's no sound!"

Mom couldn't yell backstage but she could sweat, pray, ring her hands, and harshly whisper. "Get the horse!" she told him. It was that old adage: *The show must go on.* Ben bolted for the truck.

Mom grabbed Dad's boater hat and headed for the stage. Her features were choked with strain until she hit the lights, and a serene smile spread across her face. She held the hat while Dad filled it with his endless fount of cards. Through her smile she told him he had to stall; The Vanishing Horse would be running late.

Across the stage, I spotted Al and Brody in the wings with their panel. Dad had finished the card routine, and the crowd applauded. I listened for the sound of hooves.

Dad began the horse routine with his usual opening line. "It's hoedown time!" This was the cue for the music. The sound of the waiting, shuffling audience filled the moment. The grange hall man still fiddled with the electric panel.

Dad clapped his hands together. "Come! Join the fun!"

Mom opened the curtain. The stage was empty. Silence.

"Please meet our mascot. She'll be here any moment. Frankie… Frankie." He could stall no more. We waited for Ben and Frankie. "And what a fine mascot she is. Our Frankie, yes, sir…"

I heard Mom's high heels clamoring out the stage door to find Ben and the horse. Soon after, I saw Frankie's white, four-sided diamond blaze emerging from the dark. *Clippety-clop. Clippety-clop.* She was approaching the stage with Ben solemnly holding her reins.

Halfway through the routine, Dad's voice crackled through the microphone. The sound had returned, and the music kicked in.

In the car that night Mom massaged her shoulder and whimpered, "Those boys don't know anything."

In the backseat, I puzzled over Brody's lack of concern in our moment of crisis. Now I suspect that when he realized he couldn't fix the sound equipment, he left because he simply didn't know what else to do. At the time, he appeared alarmingly indifferent. What was going on? I ran my finger along the edge of my metal-clad front teeth, bit off a fingernail, and flicked it to the floor of the car. Nerves. As we left the lights of the town, I looked down the road to the darkness ahead.

15

THE INGÉNUE AND THE WIRE LADY

I have failed to look forward to the Prom.

With Frankie, the vanishing horse

WHAT I REMEMBER ABOUT the top hat is the way it rumbled below my bottom as it rolled downstage into position, and that little smile Ben and I exchanged when he looked down at me as he spun the hat on its pedestal. Of course, jumping out of the hat was always an exquisite thrill, arms open dramatically with a debutante's exuberance.

Great forces were stirring. From theater to diner to motel, I felt infused with a new courage in myself. How much of that was genuine or a by-product of the bright, heady spotlight I can't say. I do know it was confusing to be a dreamy girl facing the possibility of big-time showbiz. Casino bookings, nightclub gigs; *television opportunities might come our way*. Things got distorted. It was hard to know what was real, or the proper way to understand my part in the magic show. I was drunk on air and light and lipstick and my sinuous figure in the scant backstage light. Because what was also true, besides changes of heart, were changes in my body. I was outgrowing my clothes. My flesh bulged against every button, strap, and zipper, tops too snug, pants too tight. I couldn't even fasten the top button of my jeans, and I broke the fragile seam of my crystal-blue satin pants while crawling into a trap. I was bursting all over, a ripe and juicy peach, squeezed into confining stitches.

In every mirror, I gawked at myself. In mirrors bordered with movie star lights, mirrors in big empty rooms with high fluorescent bulbs, mirrors in cold high school locker rooms, mirrors above sinks in old dingy bathrooms, and mirrors in every cramped place we had to dress in. I was a topography of burgeoning peaks and valleys. I had womanly curves, a va-va-va-voom figure completely out of sync with my maturity level. Mom told me to exaggerate my makeup to compensate for the powerful spotlight, and I had taken it to garish extremes—darkly outlined eyes, blazing pink cheeks, and bright crimson lips. I smeared gobs of foundation on my face for a caramel hue. Since I could never decide on one lipstick shade, I always wore a few, and they mixed together into one gooey tropical blend. All dressed up in a leotard, sequins, and black pumps with my harlot cheeks and raccoon eyes, I saw little of the rising star I thought I was. No matter how I tried, I never had Mom's casual gait in high heels. I couldn't even wear them without constantly looking down to admire my feet.

I wore my favorite costume in The Vanishing Horse, a red-striped shirt, short red overalls, and white platform boots. The boots and shorts elongated my legs, and my shiny nylons wrapped them in a coco butter tan. In my thinking this was the epitome of the go-go-girl cool I'd seen on TV. Still no sly looks from Brody. Not even Clair with her trim, compact figure interested him in that way. He had attended an all-boys Catholic school, and maybe he was as shy about girls as I was about boys.

I was plagued by questions about dating and sex. The older neighborhood girls had told me frightening tales of making out with boys and letting them feel their breasts. I wanted one of those frank talks women had with girls my age. In particular, I wanted Clair to be my confidant in such matters. In my French class they called it a *tête-à-tête*, which essentially means a private chat between friends. This would certainly make us chums.

In a dressing room in Corvallis, I broached the subject while we sat before an old vanity with buzzing yellow lights around the perimeter. As she dabbed a swab into a pool of blue eyeshadow, I dropped a leading question. "Did you have a boyfriend in college?" I said, my voice smooth as I reached for my eyeliner.

"For a while," she said, squinting at herself beneath half-closed lids. In two quick strokes her eyes sparkled in galaxy blue. I romanticized the ritual of putting on makeup each night, while Clair did it mechanically, with the passion of an overworked cocktail waitress. "He's down in L.A. now. I think," she said, artlessly smearing blush on her cheeks. "Or Phoenix."

I waited for her to elaborate. Swiping a straight line of cranberry lipstick across her mouth, she said no more. By the time she zipped up her makeup bag and stood up, I had missed my chance.

She touched her mouth, repressing a yawn. "You need help with schoolwork?" she asked.

I kept my head down and opened my case of blush with its smudged little mirror. "I'm good," I told her, my usual answer.

She marched off. I listened to her sharp tread down the hall until it faded away. Clair was my teacher. Of academics. That was all. Slowly, I dusted my cheekbones in a fuchsia color, feeling a new layer of disappointment settle into sediment. I had to search elsewhere for help, and this meant my mother. I assumed she was too old-fashioned to be very forthcoming. But watching her the last few weeks, I thought it possible all that had changed. Some of the starchy proprieties of the suburbs had worn away, and all things felt possible after seeing her transported between four contraptions in two minutes flat. In addition, there was her militant sorcery at her little table, stage right.

By then I had realized the deepest, truest secret about my father's magic show. My mother ran the show. Her table was the hub, its mission control. A heartbeat of music, props, and motion emanated from this one place, with her at the center. She drew curtains, flipped lights, ran music, and onstage delivered and retrieved all props. If anyone had a question, they went to Mom at her table. If anything important happened, they went to Mom. If catastrophe, illness, or death occurred during the show, Mom was the first to know. A desk light with a flexible neck cast a sphere of clerical yellow down on her workstation. This was where she kept the props. Once she was done with a prop, she stashed it in the ragtag hobo luggage on the floor nearby. Throughout the show, she would constantly move items in and out. Always on the right corner of her table was a big amplifier with lots of silver switches and red lights. On top of the amplifier, she kept a little mirror next to her capsule of lipstick, and a wind-up clock for keeping track of starting times and intermission. Next to the amplifier was a device for Dad's wireless mic and a cassette player. The cassettes were arranged in order of use in a Halston shoebox. Everything on her table had a place and purpose, or it was not on her table.

After my talk with Clair, I went stage right to hover nearby while Mom checked the props. Some of the props were everyday items: twine, paper, pencil, lighter, scissors, paring knife, and fluffy powder puff. All of it was as neatly arranged as the place settings of an elaborate seven-course meal. I hoped whatever advice on romance my mother shared would be as clean and tidy as her tabletop.

Peering into her little mirror, she touched up her lipstick, smacking her lips together, while I searched for a question or a statement that might broach the subject. It was more difficult than I thought. We just didn't talk about uncomfortable subjects. If I had a problem, I got fewer reassuring words, more tangible remedies—a haircut or new clothes.

Mom was writing that night's lineup on a piece of paper in her neat cursive—opening, coins, piano, rope tie, horse, three-card monte, substitution trunk, clocks, cards, backstage, bread, floating lady and ball, lemon, cannon—and then she pinned it to the curtain in front of her table. I desperately hoped she would take the initiative herself. Her only guidance for menstruation was to buy a big box of sanitary napkins, point to them one day in the cabinet, and tell me, "Here they are when you need them."

Now the situation felt urgent. My first love interest so close, my flowering body. The prospect of navigating, by myself, the complexities of boys felt overwhelming. She stood next to me, checking the tapes in her shoebox, one hand on her round hips, her red lips glistening, her skin radiating a candlelight glow. I silently willed her to speak.

Look at me. I'm changing.

Just behind us we heard chuckling. We both turned. Ben and Brody had nabbed the wire form for The Floating Lady. It was a woman's figure of wire lacework topped with a mannequin head partially concealed by a sheer veil. They tossed her back and forth with flustered faces and silly grins.

"She likes you."

"No, she likes you."

"She likes you."

I noted her pointy breasts, small waist, and trim hips and felt a sense of inadequacy. I assessed my own hip bones and fat thighs. The wire lady had no arms, sharp upright toes, legs fused together, and a hideous lady's head with a nicked face. Even though she couldn't speak or think, her exaggerated womanly curves had undeniable powers over the boys. She was defenseless and obscene in their clutches, with her empty stare and bobbing head. I wanted to destroy her and also free her from their grasp. I felt the sensation of moving fast, careening around blind corners, unpeeled and raw.

I looked at my mother. Every feature of her face conveyed exasperation—eyes flashing, and her red mouth pursed. She shook her head, deeply sighing. *Those silly boys.* Turning around, she resumed her duties. Not knowing what else to do, I followed suit. Wrapping my arms around myself, I felt small and unsure. Perhaps I sensed I was on my own. This would come to be true. As I made my way to becoming a woman, my mother would never be very open with me. She was conservative, and the changing times scared her a little. And she probably figured the sex-ed class I had at school got her off the hook. I watched the boys tote the wire lady away. I longed to spin myself up in our black curtain, turning, turning, going deeper into my own cocoon where I could stay comfortably invisible.

The last days of February slipped by as we rolled through Oregon, and I often found myself at the end of the night too excited to sleep. In numerous motel rooms, I would tell my parents I had homework to do, and set up a makeshift camp in the bathroom while they slept.

Leaning against a wall on a motel pillow, I would read or write in my journal. On those late nights, I discovered the show had left a smell on my skin. Each time I hid in the big gold top hat, I was engulfed by a peculiar scent. Lifting my arm to my nose, I inhaled again and again: sawdust, pepper, and velvet. My skin was also particularly warm. Maybe the spotlight had seeped in and now radiated out of me. Heat and smell. Vibration and light. No wonder I stayed up late in motel bathrooms. The magic show clung to me and I to it, and it was hard to give it up to sleep.

Sometimes, under frosted windows in cold-floor bathrooms, I tried to start that *Reader's Digest* article, my hand poised, unmoving across the page. All that white space screamed at me. Pressure had mounted. When Dad asked to see the article, I would tell him it wasn't ready, implying I was laboring over it. In truth, I'd written nothing. As the challenges of the road increased, I had become conflicted about the Pollyannaish story he wanted me to write. I kept thinking about the crashed truck and wayward crew, walking backstage through deep pools of light then dark, and the feel of nylon stockings under my fingertips. None of that belonged in the article.

Eventually, I would pick up my red two-hundred-page journal and write about all of that there. The big journal pulsed in my hands. I liked to flip ahead to the empty pages. Touching their white surface, I felt a quiet reverence. I wrote about everything. Dad's private stash of gimmicks in the top drawer of his trunk, and the way the spotlight would spill like a pitcher of milk into the wings. I also wrote about Dad accidentally dropping a coin in his routine, and its terrible clank and roll across the stage. How awful I felt when a little boy picked it up and paraded it around the theater.

Eventually, my thoughts would drift to Brody. In one town I stumbled across him in his ruffled shirt standing before our dressing room mirror. A court card flickered between his fingers as he presented a preening stage smile to the same invisible crowds I knew so well. My affection for him was sealed. I had also noticed a change. In his sweeping gaze, I had started to register. Across a diner table he paused for a sliver of a moment on my smeared, dark-eyed face. Or maybe it was an error of sight, an illusion of my own making.

On our day off in Salem, Mom and I took the cousins to a shopping mall and parted at the large central fountain.

"See you in two hours," she told them, and we sped off to find me new clothes that fit.

It was the first day in weeks we had time to shop, and we flipped through racks with a restrained furor. In the lingerie department, I picked out bras that swayed from the hangers in a womanly dance. At a fabric store, Mom bought two yards of gold sequin material and a sewing pattern for a wraparound vest. As my black-and-white-striped vest was too tight, Mom wanted to sew a new costume for The Opening.

"We're running late," she told me. She had to find a new leotard to match the vest, so she sent me to meet the boys.

At the fountain, I saw Brody striding toward me with Ben at his side, poking his elbows into Ben's ribs as they traded barbs. They plopped down next to me with Brody by my side, still smiling from their jabby one-liners.

"Hey," he said with a saucy light in his smoky eyes, "who's this? 'Some weasel took the cork out of my lunch!'" He was laughing at Al. I didn't want to laugh at Al, but I did, guffawing foolishly. Then he imitated Al imitating Clark Gable: "'Frankly, my dear...'" It was tainted laughter. I bit my cheeks to stop my ingratiating smirking. Being a wiseass with Brody delighted and horrified me. I didn't know I could so easily betray people I cared about. He even had a name for The Great Alexander: "The Great Cognac thinks he knows it all,"

Brody snickered. "Well, excuuuuuse me!"

We all knew Al and Brody didn't get along. Al couldn't resist giving stage instructions, even if unwelcome. *You gotta put tools back in the kit...Someone could trip in the dark, you leave those hideaway steps there...Put on that bow tie. This isn't the prom, son.*

His face straightened. "I do have something to tell you."

I turned to him, relieved he was changing the subject. I noted a little scarlet mark on his jaw where he'd cut himself shaving.

Clearing his throat in a serious way, he said, "Your mom wore her glasses onstage."

"She did?" My mouth opened in surprise.

He grinned wickedly. "Yeah, she did! She did!" He laughed, slapping his knee.

Color rose to my face. I managed a small, hesitant smile and airily brushed off his remark. "She can't see at her table that well—she forgot, that's all." We silently watched the shoppers go by. He smelled of ketchup and popcorn from his mall lunch.

"Uncle Mazzie always said your dad was so smart." He wrinkled his nose. "What's so good about that piano?"

I studied the inside of my palm to hide my irritation. The piano was fine. Our biggest problem in our magic show was Brody. He lacked zest, gumption, and good manners. Sometimes I wondered if he grasped the magnificence of our mission. Still, I was so aware of his shoulder and leg inches from mine, his slippery smile pulling me in. I was courting disaster to care. All I could feel was his unhappy, prickly presence. Next to Brody, Ben chatted with a freckled waif of a girl, showing off the same gamma-ray smile that got Clair to snap his cuff links. It was just Brody and I amid bustling hordes of shoppers.

He leaned his elbows on his knees, looking down at his sneakers. I could see the back of his oily rust-dappled hair. "I thought we'd walk in places and folks would say, 'Aren't you with the magic show that's in town?'" He grunted. "Hardly anyone showed up last night."

"No biggie," I answered, and found myself telling a lie. "We sold lots of tickets coming up." In truth, I was as disappointed as him in our turnouts. I recalled those news articles in the blue scrapbook. Standing-room-only crowds, capacity crowds, spellbound crowds, sell-outs, full houses...I wondered if Dad had shown Brody his scrapbook, too. The magic show certainly wasn't what I thought it would be. I still loved it, though, for its motion and light, the buzz of strangers in their seats, and all the ridiculous promises it made to me. I wanted Brody to love it, too. I glanced at him as he sullenly stared off into the mall, a boy kidnapped under false pretenses. *Don't give up on us.*

I nervously swept my fingers through my hair. We had to win Brody over. We needed his care, hard work, and allegiance to the magic show. One iota of neglect, and magic won't work. I felt heartened when I saw those red-and-white-speckled cards edging his shirt pocket. I recalled his earnest lessons with Dad, his secret mirror practices. I had to wake him out of his sulky reverie. "What about the cards? Are you practicing?" I asked, hopefully.

He scratched his neck. "Sort of."

A feeling of dread sunk into my body. Something about this wasn't right. Maybe Brody was one of those hoodlum boys Dad was afraid would break into his garage. Now look what had happened. Dad had invited him in, shown him his tricks, and asked for his help. I still wanted to lean over and give him a big, dry kiss.

16

SOMEONE

You no what the best part is about the show is when it's over

The Grabels with Siegfried and Roy, 1990s

THOSE VEGAS TALENT SCOUTS were not our only prospect. Dad also had a friend of a friend.

"He knows someone with connections to Reno," Dad told me as rain splattered against our motel window one morning. He crossed his arms with authority. "It's a start."

Reno was a scruffy second cousin to neon king Vegas. Most likely we couldn't be picky. A steady booking was still a steady booking. A plug from this *Someone* to Reno insiders could park the magic show at one theater.

"When's he coming?" I asked.

"Portland," he said. "Day after tomorrow." He sat on the edge of the bed, smelling of mint toothpaste from his seven-minute scrub of his new teeth. He didn't mention that his parents, Grandpa and

Grandma Grabeel, were also coming to the Portland show.

I felt a tightness in my chest. Everything was happening fast. Dad had also arranged for the show to be filmed and photographed in Napa on April 29th. I started calculating time. *Someone,* day after tomorrow. Napa, eight weeks away. Las Vegas for the Kiwanis Club, ten days later. Were we ready? Dad held the tour's itinerary, a listing of dates and theaters typed on blue-lined binder paper.

Across the room, Mom stuffed a white handkerchief in her purse and announced cheerfully, "It's Ruth Ann's birthday today. I'm going to call." Unclipping one of her big gold earrings, she picked up the phone and dialed Oklahoma.

"What we need is a publicity packet," Dad said, tapping his pen on his yellow list. He explained the packet would include video and photographs of the Napa show, and newspaper articles from reporters who had covered the show.

"That *Reader's Digest* article would be a nice addition." His cloudless blue eyes locked on me. "How's it coming?"

I traced the seam on my blue jeans.

"I can give you a few opening lines," he said in hopes of inspiring me. "You could write, 'The audience was aghast as Dad floated the piano' or 'Money doesn't grow on trees, except in Dad's clever coin routine.'" He was pleased with himself, and a little grin danced around his mouth. "What about, 'Dad proved the hand *is* quicker than the eye.'"

Inwardly, I cringed at his stale examples. My own story of the road was forming. I didn't know what it was, I just knew he would never like it. A meaningful pause unfolded as I felt him watching me. Maybe he could see all of me, all of my embarrassments and failings, the worst of me. *Whatdoyouknowyou'rejustalittlegirl.* I did know something. I had never felt so important to him before. I could not let him down.

He offered a final instruction. "When you're writing about the show, you have to use artistic license," he said, waving a finger for emphasis. "Build it up like the Empire State Building."

I shuddered. He wanted sophisticated hokum. Mom turned down a movie with John Wayne. He really shot her out of a cannon, and we lived on a ranch. As phony as it was, that story might get us a steady booking at the Sahara, the Stardust, the Sands …

I had to do it.

"You know what they say?" He tossed his pen up, and we watched its pinwheel turn in the air. "Modesty is honesty," and he caught it with a fast swipe of his hand. We both laughed. I swelled with renewed commitment. He added, "You know how your mom is shot from the cannon, right?"

I'd read the old publicity. "Spring method," I said firmly.

"Good girl."

When we arrived at the theater, I made the rounds with the news. First, Clair. I told her about the prospect of a Reno booking.

She tucked her book under her arm and exclaimed, "How exciting this is for you!" My smile froze. That's what Cindy said when she was just being polite.

Next, I told Al, who sat on a stool backstage buffing his leather shoes with a big horsehair brush. "Well, Kate, what can I tell you? You can't pick your family, but you can always pick a card."

I found Dot standing in front of the sedan's open trunk full of cotton candy supplies. When I told her about *Someone*, she flicked a speck of lint off her shoulder and said, "Like Mr. Wonderful didn't have enough problems."

We played an old vaudeville house outside of Portland. Fascinated by its antiquated grandeur, I began to roam. First, through chorus dressing rooms filled with unadorned vanities and marred foggy mirrors. Then, the veiled backstage, in and out of its puddles of murky light. A big, tangled fly loft opened up above my head, and below my feet I peered through the panels into a dark, empty orchestra pit. The house was crowned by a dome of gold leaf with lines radiating from its center, the spokes of a wheel. The entire place was softly lit with hundreds of little lights along the aisles and balconies resembling the candles on a multitier wedding cake. Most astonishing was its size. Three thousand seats that flared out from the stage in a half embrace ready to lurch and squeeze once the music started.

I headed up the center aisle, through the red-carpeted lobby, and up the curved staircase to the top balcony and sat in a seat in the far corner. I let myself melt into the expansive quiet.

My renewed commitment to the *Reader's Digest* article was already waning. I could never comfortably fit inside my father's narrative. There, in the dark, I acknowledged that the periphery of the show was far more interesting to me. Our antics and pratfalls, comings and goings, triumphs and fumbles, onstage and off—all my wild musings and analyses that trouping inspired. Those moments when the show was turned inside out, a garment with its mad, slapdash stitching exposed. All the dusty, lonely theaters we played, and the motel rooms with drawn curtains and messy beds left for other women to make. That was the story I wanted to tell. The truth of it bothered me, and I cradled my face in my palm, wondering what I was going to do about my father.

Down below on the second tier was a stain-smudged wall. Dirty water had seeped through and peeled away the plaster in chunks, leaving a continent-shaped blotch with jagged shores. I slowly took in my surroundings. Stuffing tumbled out of the mohair seat next to me. I didn't notice till then the theater's decrepit condition. Mom had told me when we arrived it was condemned, slated for the wrecking ball the following week. We were to be its last show. Three wires jutted from the wall. Maybe someone had ripped out a sconce for their living room as they were leaving a matinee.

I traipsed down the staircase with its unraveling carpet, through the dreary lobby and the center aisle with its missing lights, my step firm and heart full. I felt that good, that oblivious to the glorious wreckage surrounding me. I believed my life would be immune from rubble and ruin, disappointment and heartache, and I'd garner only success in every flavor.

Had I known the truth, I would have been devastated. The years ahead would fall short of my most fervent wishes. There'd be no rapt crowds, no fancy careers, no triumphs in elegant evening wear, just the wins and losses common to most. That's why I always remembered that condemned theater. All my big dreams would come crashing down like the theater's mortar, plaster, and stone.

When I returned backstage, the Lions Club sponsors delivered the pallet box for The Escape Box. The men and Dad stood around it.

"Looks mighty fine, fellas," Dad said and walked around it, inspecting it up and down. "Hmmm. It's going to be a hard one, I can see that." The men whooped with pleasure.

Less than ten minutes after they left, I discovered Dad hiding behind a crate tearing away a board on the lid with his claw hammer. *So that's how he did it.* He loosened the board before the show, and while inside the box, he simply slid the board away and climbed out with the tent concealing him. Then he slid it back into place.

Upon seeing him, I cried, "Dad!" It was so silly, we both laughed.

He then rested his arm on his knee. "Look at me, pretending I have good sense." He saw my delight and said, sadly, "Your ol' dad is making a bad impression on you."

He feared I was wrongly influenced by his folly. And I was. Whatever he wanted to protect me from, it was too late. I somehow loved everything about traveling with the magic show. The scorching spotlight and cool, dusty stages, the jolly blaring music, our boisterous midnight breakfasts in those diners bathed in yellow light, the moon following us through the Cadillac windows, our caravan into the night, the storied road.

He continued prying the board loose until it smoothly slid away and back in place. He told me, again, "Play it safe, Kate. Be a bank teller, teacher, or an escrow girl. Get a job with security." This was my father's biggest wish for me—secure employment. Then he stuck me in his big magic show. I laughed out loud. It was such an absurd notion: me, becoming just another boring adult, mired in mediocrity.

The Portland theater had all the amenities to impress *Someone*. A proper glossy pine floor and draped stage, thick-cushioned seats, and a big follow spotlight ready to pan and tilt as needed. After arriving, we stayed long enough to ensure that our backdrop was hung and the crew on track with their duties.

"We want a smooth show tonight," Dad told Al before we jumped in the Cadillac for my grandparents' house.

Dad didn't appear eager to visit them. His career as a stage magician had puzzled his parents from the start. All my father's success in manning a traveling magic show did not offset my grandparents' worries over my parents' vagabond life. Years ago, when Portland replaced trolleys with buses, Grandpa got a route through the city. Each time he saw the magic show, he would say, even as the last happy audience members were leaving the theater: "I can get you a job down at the bus depot."

Grandpa loved visiting the Lee Grabel Realty office with Dad's desk in the back, ringing phones, and salespeople bustling in and out. During their visits they cavorted with Dad, from putting green to lunch. Sometimes Grandpa and Dad played golf, and Grandma drove the cart. They always returned home hooting about Grandma's crazy driving. As she never learned to drive a car, the cart was her big toy, and she was known for her fast breaks and wide turns off the path. She loved being the terror of the fairway. Dad also drove his parents to the houses he sold, where they would jump out of the car and pose on the curb for a photograph. Sometimes they went to the office and did the same thing. Grandma would pretend to be the secretary, sitting at Mom's desk, talking on the phone while Dad snapped a photo. Or Grandpa would sit at Dad's desk, shuffling paper while Grandma pretended to take dictation. Then they would hop in the car to drive by a new listing or to Dad's Chamber of Commerce meeting. Mom stayed out of their way. My grandparents thought she was incredibly extravagant with Dad's money, and she thought them incredibly cheap. My mother and grandmother still harbored hurt feelings from incidents that happened before I was born.

As we drove to my grandparents' house before the Portland show, a light rain spotted the windshield. We passed through a neighborhood of little pre-war houses with tidy porches and pitched roofs, and then parked in front of a white clapboard house. The mailbox read "Grabeel."

Dad had called them before we left and minimized the entire venture. "Something came up...Just a few shows, nothing big... See you in Portland." Now that we were here with our magic gear, they would see this was no casual sojourn with a rabbit and a hat.

Inside, we sat in the kitchen as Grandpa stuffed his pipe with tobacco and Grandma poured cups of coffee. She said primly, "I didn't fix anything fancy."

It might have been a subtle dig at Mom. Mom sipped her coffee and commented on the flowers out the window. "I see your dahlias are coming along."

Grandma offered me juice, milk, pop. No, no, no. She offered me ice cream. No. Then she placed a dinner plate of cookies in front of me. I didn't move. Mom complained so much about her, I felt uncomfortable showing her affection.

The cookies remained untouched. "Hmph," she said, perplexed. She sat down in an unladylike fashion with her legs apart and her arms resting on her thighs. "I'm all plucked out," she muttered.

Grandpa sat at the kitchen table, puffing on his pipe. "Whatcha doing out there again, Merle?" he asked flatly.

Dad nimbly evaded his question: "No worries, just a little tour. I'll be back at work soon." Maybe I would have believed him if I didn't know the truth. Grandpa kept on, unconvinced of his assurances.

"You're a grown man now," he said, wetting the pipe stem. "You got another child and your office. You're going to lose your shirt if you keep playing with these toys." Grandpa didn't sound angry. He had lost the tonal inflection of his voice, and his sage warning had the urgency of an oil-change recommendation.

Dad shoved his hands in his pockets and started to drift around the kitchen, following a secret current.

Grandma let out a little whimper. We turned our heads. She was twisting a paper napkin into a knot. "Oh, mighty," she sniffled.

I suspect a part of Grandma was very proud of Dad's magical talents. She just didn't think a magic show was worth risking the luxuries of life for. Her face crumbled into tears. "This is a doozy!"

Mom retrieved a handkerchief from her purse and handed it to her.

"We're just fine," Dad crooned, touching her shoulder. "We still have the business, the house. Nothing has changed." After that she wiped her eyes, feeling better that my parents' solvency was intact and that the golf course's fleet of glossy-white battery-charged carts would be waiting for her on their next visit.

Grandpa took the pipe out of his mouth to say something important. "I don't have to tell you how hard it is out there, Merle. You got a little security now. Play it safe." Dad had just told me those same words. I glanced at him as he touched the watch on his wrist and stopped himself from looking at it.

Before we left, Dad's mouth curved into a grin, and he called Grandma by her moniker. "Ol' pedal to the metal Gracie," he teased, and the heavy mood shifted.

"We got tri-tip and the fixings to go with it," Grandma told us. "Bring everyone back after the show."

During the show that night, I peeked through the curtain a lot, scanning faces, trying to pick out *Someone.* I also kept a keen eye on my grandparents in their aisle seats. Sometimes I'd see their small stony faces floating on the soft blurry edges of the spotlight. I wondered if I'd caught them momentarily expressionless. I figured The Escape Box had to please them, as Dad's appearance at the back of the theater was packed with style and surprise. Even so, during the number I was bewildered to see their same straight faces when he made his triumphant stride past their seats to the stage.

After the show, I dressed and searched for *Someone* amid the folks waiting around the stage. A family with small kids asked for Dad's autograph. I caught Dad on his way back to his wardrobe trunk. "Was he here?"

"He gave his tickets to his sister and her family." He jerked his head toward the parents and kids who had wanted his autograph. His lower lip puffed out. "What good does that do us?" We both shared the sighs of noble sages in a world of imbeciles.

I walked down to the seats where my grandparents awaited us. When Grandma saw me, she clambered out of her seat and fondled my shoulder. Her perfume encased me, while her little figure was lost in her long paisley dress. I was used to her trying to wiggle into my affections, and I thought she would tell me she loved my costumes and how beautiful I was onstage. Her soft pink face hovered near me as I prepared to savor her fawning praise. She stroked the top of my head, my strands of fine hair catching her fingers.

In a trembly voice she said, "Poor Katy. You're going to lose everything."

After the show, at my grandparents' kitchen table, I wondered what she meant. Maybe she thought I had been forced to join lowly show folk, and now I'd never have a nice car or walk-in closet or shiny white washer and dryer.

Watching her happily refilling coffees, enjoying the Pocus Posse's jesting, I felt a jolt of confusion. I was ready to leave Portland. My grandparents' fears and the broken promise of *Someone* had carried their share of discouragement. Perhaps Dad felt that way, too. He was eyeing the kitchen clock, waiting for a tactful moment to make our exit. The road was calling.

17

AWOL

It' seems so sad about this poor man. Almost ~~was~~ 60 years old, still dreaming about a how to bring ~~in~~ his show up to the fame & recognition it god damn deserves. Well, take me out of school! Send that tape to Vegas! Pound at them until they see it & pound more to get what you want! Do it <u>now</u>! Don't let me & my education stop you!

Showgirl Katy on stage, 1977

AFTER SEVEN WEEKS ON tour, I was so smitten with the magic show, I launched a clandestine coup of my mother's backstage duties. In a high school theater in La Grande, I leaned toward her powdered, fluttering figure. "Anything you want me to do?" I whispered, eager and breathless in her small halo of work light where she captained the show. She hardly noticed my offer as she deftly changed music with an index finger pressing hard on the play button. "No, honey," she said, her eyes never lifting from the props she bundled and unbundled. I languished by her side, disappointed she didn't take me more seriously. I was bored with slipping on and offstage while the magic show hummed under her fingers.

Once we landed that Vegas booking, a bigger role for me in the show wouldn't be an impossible notion. I thought my mother might grow to love that white stucco house in Vegas I imagined us living in, once she applied her homemaking skills to it. I hoped she would willingly acquiesce her stage duties to me for blooming hibiscuses, pretty bed sheets, and new living room furniture.

Peeking over her bare shoulder, I felt myself poised to usurp her in my oozy lipstick. "Well, just in case. I'm here if you need anything," I purred.

I got nowhere. She wasn't being territorial. She took her duties too seriously to trust me or anyone else. During The Cannon finale that night, I stood like a soldier at my post while she dashed onstage in her tunic of streaming, shimmering silver, a mercurial space-age queen in liquid metal. Beneath my big smile, I sulked. To be the Human Cannonball was the real catch. I felt a wistful longing as she zipped across the stage into the arms of Ben and Brody, who, with a heave-ho, loaded her into the barrel. *I could do that.* I noticed her jog across the stage was more steady than fast. My reign was inevitable. In the harsh reality of showbiz, I had youth on my side.

"I can do The Cannon," I offered her the next night. "In case you're tired, or something." Looking at me over her assembly line of props, she gave me the same pained expression as when I told her I didn't want to move to Oklahoma. Maybe she had realized her pixie little fourteen-year-old was vying to replace her.

"Sweetie, I got it," she firmly said. I never mentioned it again.

I spent the rest of the night in our cramped little dressing room practicing The Look before a mirror. At least in the magic show, I got to tell folks I was in showbiz. And sometimes the spotlight panned across my feet.

When we got to Washington, a trick just as good as The Cannon came my way—The Floating Lady. A change in the show's lineup prevented Clair from doing the trick, and I stepped in as a handy solution.

The Floating Lady was different from other routines. No smiles or jaunty music. It had an overwrought dreamy quality with violins, dim moody darkness, and Dad dramatically posing with one arm reaching up, fingers splayed, to defy gravity. Dad liked this illusion because he felt it was unlike other floating lady numbers. He had given it an original touch by adding the mannequin head to the wire form.

I wore a long, stiff, white chiffon dress, silver flats, and a sheer white veil that draped across my nose and mouth. Slowly, I would walk onstage. A blue spot, strategically pointing away from the strings, illuminated the stage in lunar light and cast small crater-shaped shadows on Dad's face. When I stood before him, he really hoked up all that mumbo-jumbo voodoo drama and even put a little muscle into it, dancing his arms around. "Hocus Pocus," he would chime with his microphone off, as Brody and I concealed our chuckles. I would fall back with eyes closed into Brody's outstretched arms. I felt his hands on my back. Cool. Certain. Every motion magnified. Then Dad was at my feet, lifting me up along with Brody. As they laid me down on the table, a white silken sheet concealed me for a moment. That's when I rolled into the concave space of the table. In my place Dad set the wire lady, which had been hidden away on a back shelf of the table, and swiftly covered it with the white sheet. When the lady started to rise, I was pushed away in the table.

From backstage I would watch the rest of the illusion, fascinated by the sight of my floating self. The wire lady was shorter than me, at least by six inches, and her feet smaller, about a size five. We were both mousy brunettes with matching makeup: red lips, pink cheeks, eyes outlined in black. A few sooty smudges sullied her milky complexion, making her appear even more forlorn than she already was. It was hard to imagine the crowd mistaking the wire lady for a real woman, except for the fact the stage was dark and the white veil concealed half her face.

Dad would raise her high into the dusty blue light and lower her back down. He then prepared for the ending. He would cover the mannequin head with the white sheet, and within that sheet was a black bag that concealed the head completely. Hovering his hands over the sleeping lady, she appeared to be floating on his fingertips, when actually, he was cutting the strings. He would then walk toward the audience, delicately holding the wire form between his fingers.

For the finale, four things happened at once. First, Dad threw the wire lady against the backdrop while the floodlights were turned on to blind the audience. This prevented them from seeing the wire form on the floor. Then the curtain quickly closed. And lastly, Al made a big noise backstage by shooting a blank into a cap from a sawed-off shotgun. The same *Bang!* he produced for The Cannon. The ending to The Floating Lady was a fast round of misdirection tactics—bright lights, loud noise, and a swiftly closing curtain.

After the number, the wire lady lay on a black woolen cloth on the floor upstage, just a discarded dress form from a seamstress's junk pile.

Each night, I watched Ben pick her up off the stage floor, her shapely mutant body handled so carelessly by the collarbone, waist, thighs, butt, and carried away.

I was too stage-struck to contemplate this weird objectifying of my gender in the show. From what I had seen on television, all magic shows did this. Women were vanished, produced, transported, levitated—moved around, here and there, like an exclamation point. For all that staged powerlessness, as a daughter of a magic duo, I sensed that the story was incomplete. Offstage, my mother wasn't particularly helpless or my father particularly powerful. And I certainly loved my part in the drama. If my father had wanted to feature me in a Burned Alive, Decapitation, Sawing, or Bullet Catch, I would have been thrilled.

Although happy to be starring in The Floating Lady, I didn't want Clair disappointed she had lost her featured trick, replete with soft lulling music, hazy blue spot, and the chance to show off her inner actress by feigning a hypnotic coma. In a dressing room in Walla Walla, as I changed out of my floating-lady dress, I regarded Clair across the room. The dressing room had a spongy orange carpet, and the garbage cans brimmed with food wrappers and bottles from high school students who had performed a play over the weekend. Clair was already dressed for the next act, reading a book with her spine as erect as a pencil.

"I'm sorry about The Floating Lady," I offered.

Her face lit up with surprise. "Why?"

"You're not doing it anymore," I explained.

She widened her eyes at my silly apology. "That costume is itchy. And it smells in the table."

As I slipped the white dress on a hanger, I pondered whether Clair even liked being in the magic show. She was mysteriously unimpressed by us. Maybe she was too practical to be lured into the show's seductions and spells. In almost every theater, I would see her backstage reading the fire escape directions. In The Floating Lady her entrance onstage had been stiff, cautious, her eyes searching the floor for banana peels. My Floating Lady had much more depth. In the trance of fluid darkness, I had to surrender to larger forces, forgo all demands. I understood the floating lady deep inside.

I had assumed that once in our show Clair would dump her dreams of working in a school. Now I wasn't so sure. "Are you really going to be a teacher?" I couldn't keep the alarm out of my voice.

"Sure am," she answered, bending down to zip up her boots.

I imagined her merrily correcting papers with her books and

teacher's manuals neatly stacked, a coffee mug on her desk. I couldn't believe she didn't want to dazzle a crowd, to be toasted with leaded crystal goblets.

"How's that math?" Clair asked, fiddling with her alphabet necklace. I told her fine.

She walked over and stood by my chair. I saw her hand on the backrest, her nails painted white, as iridescent and shiny as the underside of little fish. When she spoke her voice was soft and concerned. "Katy, I haven't helped you at all."

A few weeks ago, I'd started guessing at the equations. Each time she returned from an outing with the cousins and asked, "How's school?" I dismissed her offer. This was payback for being excluded from their friendly chatter, for her treating me like a kid. My algebra book, with its loose spine and puzzling symbols, was the only thing she wanted from me. I began a silent campaign to refuse her efforts. In the dressing room that night, under her pointed gaze, I kept my head down, for fear she'd see my defiance. I could feel her eyes probing me, trying to will my cooperation.

"Tomorrow when we get to the theater, show me where you're at," she said crisply.

The next day Clair and I had our first math session at a cavernous National Guard armory near Vancouver. After we dragged in the proscenium, erected it, and set up the show, we sat cross-legged center stage next to a miniature scholastic city of stacked textbooks, pencils, and paper. She had pushed away her bangs with yellow barrettes as if ready for a spirited bout of spring cleaning.

Pointing at numbers in my math book, she began a quantitative address on reciprocals and products, which, from what I gathered, once mingled together, fractionated down into near air.

Squeezing my lips, I stared at the numbers, unable to focus. She kept looking at me, pointing at the page. Masquerading as a showgirl must have been excruciating for her all these weeks, and now she could let her teaching acumen shine.

"The reciprocal of 4 is 1/4. The reciprocal of 2/3 is 3/2. The reciprocal of 1 is 1." She was leaning in, eager for me to absorb her words. For the first time, I really had her attention.

"I understand," I said unconvincingly so she would know I was fibbing.

She announced our study schedule. We would continue to meet after setting up the show in whatever stage we were. The following day, we sat on the bleachers of a high school gym in Olympia. She wanted to know if I needed help in math. No. Help with other subjects? No.

"Just let me know when you're ready." She opened her book and I opened mine. Her canvas bag rested by her feet. A wrinkle in the bag twisted the vegetable person into a gnarled figure in rioting carrot gear. For the next few shows we camped out on different stages. On bleachers or metal fold-out seats or sitting cross-legged on hard stage floors. Every now and then she would ask me if I needed help and I'd say no.

Then one day, I abandoned study time. In a clammy little theater in Port Angeles, I fled to the Cadillac for the afternoon, pleased and guilty I had escaped her. Listening to an eight-track on the car radio, I tried to do math, skipping what I didn't understand. Most of the time, I watched dark clouds shroud the theater's tall fly loft. My junior high had made no rigorous academic demands on this trip. They were more amused that I was traveling in my father's magic show than concerned about my studies. I was pretty much assured my diploma just by handing in the work I did.

In the next few towns, I didn't show up for study time. I don't know on how many stages Clair waited for me until she figured I wasn't coming back. Then, in a wind-scrubbed theater on the coast, I walked into a small tile bathroom to change for the show and felt a definite chill across the room. Clair stood at our wardrobe trunk yanking open the drawers with her face fisted up tight. We both wiggled into our pantyhose, snapped up our matching vests, tied our little scarves—without a word. She bolted out of the room. I held my sequin makeup bag, listening to the silence in her wake. It was different. Complete and severe. I honestly hadn't thought my sly evasion would anger her. I stood before the dingy bathroom mirror, feeling shaky. What had I done?

Clair complained to Dot that I was avoiding her help. Dot told Mom and me about it at her cotton candy stand somewhere in Seattle. It was April 1st, and we'd been on the road almost two months.

With hands on hips and eyes afire, Dot declared, "Clair said, 'Katy doesn't want me to teach her.' And I said, 'Well, maybe Katy doesn't think you're a good teacher!'"

My heart dropped. That wasn't it at all. Words stuck in my throat.

"She's not a very good teacher; that's it," Mom concluded definitively.

Mom thought Clair was "anti-establishment." This meant Clair was one of those Berkeley hippies who disapproved of my parents' sensible values, two-story house, and regular hygiene. She put her arm around me to protect me from Clair, the communist bra-burning radical. "You're a good student on your own!"

I drew in my breath, alarmed by the mess I had caused.

Dot nudged me. "You don't need her help," she said with pleasure.

After that, Clair changed. Onstage, her smile flickered on and off like a bad light bulb. She usually rode with Dot at night, leaving me alone in the Cadillac to contemplate her empty space, conspicuous with mutual injury. In the long afternoon hours before the show, her vanishing act was complete. Slinging her purse over her shoulder, she would barrel out a stage door, not returning until showtime. That was okay. Her presence reminded me that I had failed her in some way.

18

ROAD SHOW RUNNING ON EMPTY

tell my in my job aplication that i worked for a maghion. That i was in show buisness, a performed. That i ~~am~~ have the ability to be able to do the show because in magic your under alot of stree and theirs many things to do, then at that moment, if not your dead. *I can alws*

Lee told the artist he wanted to look
like Uncle Sam and Jesus Christ

I SAT MISERABLY IN the center of collective anger. Our dinner with Al and Dot had erupted into a slew of indictments against Ben and Brody.

"Ben disappears right before the show starts to use the bathroom," Mom said. "The curtain is about to open and he's buttoning up his pants!" She poked her fork in the air. "He's got valve problems!"

Then Dot grumbled about Brody. "He's not wearing his bow tie anymore. He looks like a dressed-up valet parker!"

Al piped in. "I reach for a wrench and it's not there. This show isn't running efficiently, and inefficient shows are slow shows," he said in an ominous tone.

I swallowed hard. A slow road show could miss one date, then another, and an entire tour could be scrapped.

We were at a seafood restaurant in Everett on a night off, complaining over plates of fish and chips, bouillabaisse, and clam linguine. I twisted my napkin in a long spindle and tried to block out the rising crescendo of gripes. Overhead, a mounted marlin gazed into murky, unknown depths. Our funny, well-meaning boys. Our unmindful, careless boys. I loved and hated them. The road to Vegas had been packed with more trouble than all its regal court cards.

I was grateful when Dad set down his glass and restated the cardinal Rule of the Road. "We have to get along," he counseled. More distressing to him was Hank the Magician, who, Mr. Bly said, was in Utah. "Maybe he'll go broke on the Mormons," Dad moaned.

By the end of the meal, Al and Dad leaned their heads together with an air of hushed confidentiality. "I have the letter," Dad said, forcefully jabbing the air with his finger while Al gravely nodded his head. Snatches of private conversation came my way. The ranch, a tour of the Baltics, a magician named Dante. Dad was a "successor" to something. I wanted to know more, my pen itching to record every tad of Pocus Posse talk. Then Dad saw my curious head turned his way and quit talking.

The following night, we played a high school stage with sticky floors from spilled sodas, and wads of flattened gum on the vanities. Tacked on the wall was a poster from the Broadway hit *Cabaret*. Backstage, I watched Brody practicing his cards, his open palm flapping, jacks and deuces floundering in his grip.

We set up the show, trotting about, rigging props and running black thread until we were done. Then we fled from each other. Ben and Brody to the truck, Clair to explore the neighborhood, and Al and Dot to their sedan to run errands around town. Our trio retreated stage right into a triangular stronghold within the draped equipment to wait till showtime.

That night, as I lay in another motel bed, an ambulance siren pierced the night. Within its wail I heard a warning. Not all was right. It didn't matter that we'd skirted mutiny and thwarted conflict, and still not missed a show. I couldn't shake my apprehension. We had many more weeks to go before the Vegas show. So much could happen or not happen at all.

How right I was.

"Where's Ben?" Mom asked with a disapproving frown.

We were playing a small, dank stage outside of Spokane, about to start the second half, and Dad was parading around gathering coins from the dappled light and dropping them in a champagne bucket. The show had been running smoothly, tight and oiled without a hiccup or hitch. Mom's table was in order and her lipstick fresh. She was even humming a little to the music, a bouncy tune that loosened her shoulders and hips. Then she noticed Ben wasn't in the wings waiting for his cue. Irritation stamped her face. Where was he?

She craned her neck, searching the shadows. He had to be onstage soon to roll out a table for the next act. Mom and Ben had different perspectives about cues. For Mom, it was a matter of life or death. No calamity would have stopped her from being onstage to deliver a rope, hat, lock, or hammer. The theater could be on fire and overrun with stage union bosses, and she would trample over them to hand Dad a prop on time. And before doing it, she always stood in the wings a few minutes early and waited with her entire body, every bone, muscle, and eyelash, alert and ready. Most of the time, she was a wreck backstage. From the moment the music started she grunted, scowled, stomped her feet, and fretted over tasks that had never gone wrong. Although my mother was not religious, had she ever prayed, it probably would have been backstage. Ben, on the other hand, would simply wait in the stage left shadows, then stroll onstage at the right time. Mom hated that. She had told him many times to wait for his cue early in the wings so she would know he was there. He continued to saunter out at the last second.

On this night her patience gave out. She loudly whispered toward stage left. "Ben!" No response. Anger crisscrossed her brow. She took off with a cry: "Heavens to Betsy!" I heard the *clap clap* of her heels receding into the darkness. I waited. Then I saw Ben rush to the wings, his heels licked by fire.

"I had to go back there and drag him out!" Mom told Dad in the car that night, as he leaned on the wheel.

"Strength give me! Strength give me!" he wailed.

He was slowly driving out of the theater's parking lot, inching along, too overcome with emotion to focus on anything else. Two weeks earlier, while setting up The Floating Lady during the show, Brody had broken the string and they'd had to switch the lineup in the middle of the show.

Dad wasn't getting enough sleep. In the dashboard light I could see his face had drooped and his mouth had flattened. On days off, he rested in bed all afternoon to replenish his energy. That night after our diner breakfast, Dad turned away from the funny banter and rubbed his eyes. His white hair was long on the collar. As soon as the bill came, he rushed us out the door. "I need my sleep, kids," he exclaimed.

We sped to the next town. From the backseat, I saw the speedometer read eighty miles per hour.

"You'll get a ticket," Mom warned.

"I'm not getting my eight hours!" he said as the white lines flew by and a waning moon bobbed over the treetops.

Mom shook her head. "Lee, you never got eight hours on the road."

In the motel room that night, Dad prepared for sleep. He hung the Do Not Disturb sign outside, and placed the phone off the hook. On his bedside table he put the G-U-N and the yellow list. The front-desk clerk had agreed to let us have the room until eleven—an hour past checkout. Dad took part of a yellow pill.

At ten o'clock the next morning, a maid loudly knocked. And knocked again. "Maid service! Maid service!"

Dad threw back the covers, sped to our motel door, and banged on it. "Why did you do that?! Why did you do that?!" he cried. He flung it open. I heard running, a cart rattling, and his deranged query. "We have another hour! One more hour!" A maid in a starched working dress was having the shock of her life. Mom and I clawed ourselves out of sleep, barely grasping what had happened. *Did he just chase a maid? Down the hall? In his pajamas?*

He stomped back to the room and flopped down on the bed. "Strength give me!" he cried and threw the covers over himself.

Silence. Not a sound in the hall. I didn't even hear a car outside. The whole town waited to see what Lee Grabel would do next. I turned to look at him. A lump in the bed. I hid my face in the sheets, squeezing my eyes shut, waiting for someone to say something. Soon Dad threw back the blanket and scratched his ear. "What the heck."

"Still didn't get enough sleep?" Mom said, pulling herself up on an elbow.

He grumbled and headed for the bathroom, his white hair in revolt all over his head. Mom and I dressed and packed. Apparently, we were going to pretend Dad had not just chased a maid down the hall. We had to be at the theater by noon. As he sat on the bed scribbling a new list, I watched for signs of instability. He had combed his hair and buttoned his shirt. I even smelled toothpaste. His fit had passed. Leaving the room was hard. The motel maids peeked at us from behind their carts on our long walk to the elevator.

Dad slipped behind the wheel of the car, adjusted the rearview mirror, and announced, "Stress management is for sissies."

I watched the passing storefronts: insurance office, shoe repair, stationery store...Scrunched up in the corner of my seat, I felt the stirrings of an ungovernable new force. It was the road. It had turned my father into a crazed maid chaser.

I started counting. Nineteen days till the Napa filming, a month till Las Vegas.

Mom looked out the window and sighed. It was her only real response to the misadventures of the morning. Perhaps it was hard for her to find words in her sea of feelings. While Dad's mood fluctuated, Mom's steady presence reassured me. Her sharp wool blazers remained as changeless as her even disposition. Peering into the visor mirror, she checked her lipstick—still red and fresh. Everywhere she went, she stamped glassware and coffee mugs with the family crest of her red lipstick. She pushed up the visor and said, "A tornado touched down near home. I wonder how everyone is."

By the time we rolled into Yakima, we needed a day off. We had peanuts, beer, and hooch in our room and invited the crew over for drinks. Al was our bartender, whistling and picking up ice cubes with Mom's crab tongs. He poured each of us a drink. Dad, his good single malt whiskey; Mom, bourbon; and the boys, beer. Al cracked the bottle lids off with his little pinkie extended like a blue blood. Dot said, "Give me some of that giggle water," and he poured her a Chablis. Clair wanted Dad's good whiskey and held her glass as dainty as a teacup.

Al poured a can of cola into my glass in one long, flowing stream. "I'm going to eighty-six you if you cause any trouble tonight." Then he knocked his glasses askew and grabbed the wine bottle by the neck, impersonating a drunkard about to take a swig. "Cheap booze does not have to be inexpensive," he slurred.

On the edge of the bed, holding his beer, Brody imitated the sound of the ball on the string in that noisy floating ball trick. That was it, exactly. "Zrrrrrrrrr." We recognized the sound and laughed.

Dad tossed a few nuts into his mouth and said, "Maybe I'll whistle onstage and hope they don't catch on!"

"Why bother?" Al said. "The truck is loaded and so is your audience. They won't notice a thing!"

We howled with abandon, our mouths agape and teeth bared.

It was close to dinnertime. The cousins and Clair left for the free happy-hour buffet in the motel bar. The rest of us gathered up our purses and sweaters for a dinner reservation.

Mom tapped Al on the chest. "We couldn't do this without you. We couldn't do this without you." She sounded emotional. It was the bourbon and the stress of the tour.

Al shrugged. "It's amazing I still remember how to break down that piano."

"He can't take a compliment," Dot said, lighting a cigarette. "But I *know*, Helene."

Mom sat down on the bed, her body deflated of all the verve and black coffee kick that had kept her going.

"The boys just don't get it," she said bleakly.

Ben and Brody strolled to their cues instead of jogged. Without bow ties or ironed shirts, they resembled disheveled bridegrooms. They didn't worry enough about what could go wrong in a magic show. Too casual, uninspired, unmasterful in their duties. They lacked—yes, it was true—*gusto!*

I imagined the cousins and Clair right then, laughing it up over little paper plates of celery sticks and mugs of cheap beer in the motel bar. I wanted to join their fun and scold them, all at the same time. I flopped down into a chair by the window, unable to reconcile my conflicting emotions of anger and affection for Ben and Brody. This was one reason why I could never write that *Reader's Digest* story. I didn't know how to write around the show's problems.

Al turned his glass slowly in his hands, telling us that during the show Ben sometimes wandered away. When he asked Ben where he went, he said outside to look at the night sky. It didn't seem right, this wandering away. What if disaster struck onstage and we needed him? What if Ben lost track of the time and missed a cue? We gazed at the floor, stumped. Ben's actions were reckless, certainly, and rather suspicious. Dad rubbed his chin, more worried about Ben than about that noisy floating ball.

Then a shadow fell across Al's face. "I think Brody intentionally broke the strings of The Floating Lady the other night," he said.

We gasped.

"So he wouldn't have to do the trick," Al said.

The air in the motel room suddenly felt stagnant, redolent with the smells of sweat, liquor, and our fear.

"He's as temperamental as a showgirl," he said.

I held my head to squelch my burning rage. Saboteur. Traitor. Right here in the Broadway Magical Mystery Extravaganza! I glanced at Dad, my comrade in arms. We had to get the boys in line. He was evaluating us from under his wispy eyebrows, trying to decide who was the biggest threat—us or Brody. He reiterated the most important

Rule of the Road. "We have to get along."

A few shows later, Mom completed my new wraparound gold sequin top. In a small windowless room before showtime, I carefully took it out of its bag and held it in my hands. It shimmered with the breath of a living thing.

All around me were old theater props. A cardboard moon sprinkled with silver glitter, a throne of plywood spray-painted metallic gold. I slipped my long arms into the top's fiery folds; a resplendent yellow milky way enveloped me, sparkling and dancing across my chest and torso. Next, I stepped into glossy orange high heels and tied a big flouncy pumpkin-colored sash around my waist in a big bow, which bounced on my hip as I trotted to the mirror. I took a long, pleased look. A real spangled show girl smiled back at me.

When I sashayed out the door, Ben was walking by. He noticed right away and flashed me one of his big, lavish smiles. "Look at you!"

His praise pumped me up and in a spurt of bravery, I jumped in Brody's path as he walked by. "What do you think?" I gushed, spreading out my arms for a better view. His eyes lit up. His mouth opened. I could see a little joke flitting around inside. I felt myself opening, drapes pulled back. I quit breathing.

Then I heard Al stage left, exasperated. "Brody!" He had run afoul of Al again, maybe forgetting to return a tool to the kit. Brody's smile vanished. Irritation flared red and hot across his face. To my question he gave his firm and decisive opinion. First, he inspected me up and down. Face, breasts, hips, legs. "Ugly," he said and marched off.

I retreated to the dressing room and crumpled up in a chair next to a stage flat of a riverbank from *Huckleberry Finn*. My eyes stung with tears. If I'd grown up with sibling ribbing, his remark might not have hurt as much. I looked down at my pitiful tummy, big floppy boobs, my lanky legs. That's what Brody said. Ugly. I got stuck on that word, as it looped around and around my thoughts in nightmarish proportions. I could no longer overlook his shoddy work in the magic show. Suddenly, every cell in my body throbbed with anger. I had crossed over into the country where jilted lovers lived.

That night after the show, we left the theater for a local diner. "Follow me!" Dad called out to the crew. When Al backed up the truck, it started going down an embankment. People standing around the loading dock called out in alarm. Al didn't hear them. *Thump.*

The truck was in a ditch. The tractor twisted away from the trailer like a crooked loaf of white bread.

Dad flew out of the Cadillac. Ben and Brody had not helped Al.

They should have been signaling Al and guiding him when he put the truck in reverse.

Dad's face was red and pulpy, his arms flailing about as he yelled. "Why weren't you there! You're supposed to help!"

In the backseat of the Cadillac, I turned away.

"He didn't tell us he needed help!" Brody yelled back.

"THAT'S YOUR JOB!" he bellowed.

Mom put her hand to her mouth. "Oh, Lee."

He kept on yelling. Finally, I turned around. The boys were gazing down at their feet. It was awful seeing Dad unleash his temper on them, and most awful was the savage joy it brought me.

19

MAGICIAN'S LAMENT

Wanderlust = strong or unconquerable longing
for or impulse toward wandering,

Frankie on the grass with truck and Cadillac in background.

EACH TIME DAD SAID, "Strength give me," I knew he wasn't talking to God. He called on another, more relevant, power—the great Houdini up in the sky watching over our magic show of unreliable assistants.

Dad never considered himself to be in the same category as Harry Houdini because Houdini was an escape artist and not a magician. People were always blurring the distinction and fixing Dad for much older than he was by asking him if he knew Houdini, whose glory days were before Dad was born. One story defined Houdini to me—his death. Someone gave him an unfair sucker punch in the stomach before he had time to brace his abdomen muscles, and he died of peritonitis. This incident inspired gushy, big-hearted feelings in me toward little Houdini. I didn't understand what an arrogant self-promoter he had been, only that he was a brilliant, kindly man who had suffered unjustly in the hands of ruffians.

I liked to imagine Houdini looking after our caravan as we traveled from town to town, but on this night, I did not feel his dark cape of stars above me. Without the protection of Houdini, our big mission felt less ordained, just a wild punch at the world. No great dead magician could deliver us our dreams.

After Dad's rant at the boys, a tow truck pulled the trailer out, and we drove to a diner nearby. Staring out the window at the passing town, I saw only Dad's fire-spewing face in the dark streets. It couldn't get worse. Maybe Dad would call off the tour. Up ahead in the driver's seat he was quiet, looking less enraged than remorseful. He had his finger across his mouth, absorbed by the consequences of his outburst. Maybe he worried the boys would hitchhike or catch a bus back home. The underlying fear of trouping was always that we'd be abandoned mid-tour without the manpower to continue. On that night, it felt possible.

We pulled up to a diner with gravy-yellow light spilling from the windows. I flinched when I thought of us crammed together at a sticky table, pretending everything was okay. As soon as we got there, Clair bounded out of Dot's car into the restaurant, barreling past the booths to the bathroom. Outside in the parking lot, Dot loudly whispered to Mom, "I'm so glad he did that."

When they climbed out of the truck, Dad immediately back-pedaled with the cousins, pulling them over to the side to repeat the Rules of the Road in a nicer way.

The boys didn't eat with us that night, preferring we deliver them their food in the truck. I walked out there with an order of ribs and a sloppy Joe and saw Brody waiting for me in the doorway of the sleeper cab. A big down jacket overwhelmed him, his arms and upper body encased in a protective shield of puffy nylon. I handed the food to him. His gray eyes of glass and cinder met mine.

I turned around, watching my feet as I hurried across the pebbled concrete, my swishing corduroys whispering what I dared not say. *I want to go home.* My dismay clouded the night air. Was the tour that bad? I thought of my bedroom with its private stage, all my merry shenanigans never to be seen by anyone. What was wrong with pretending? Who said we had to make our dreams come true? Within my room's four walls, my imagination would never disappoint me. It was safe there, with my spinning records and the mirror that opened into worlds that only I could see. Perhaps it was enough.

I smelled springtime in the air. Out there in the darkness, the rivers rushed with snowmelt and wildflowers bloomed in the meadows. I was unsure of the town we were in and of the next town we were heading to. I didn't know the date or day of the week. Everything behind me had blurred into a jumble of hotels, theaters, and diners.

From across the parking lot, I saw the rest of the crew in the diner window, everyone making polite chit-chat as they stirred their coffees. We were not the Pocus Posse without the cousins, just a hobbled bunch of troupers with maple syrup on our fingers and yolk marks on our sleeves. I still wanted to believe in a crew's honorable duty to support its magician. I still wanted to believe in the wellspring of hope that we offer each other in the name of our dreams, yet I could not deny the icy misgivings swelling up inside of me.

Come on, boys, we need you.

Sometimes in our motel room late at night, I would think about the boys tucked inside the truck's cab in deep, mindless slumber that prevailed through the same wailing sirens and after-hours hot-rodding that always woke my parents and me. After Dad's tirade, I suspected the boys joined me in the fractured night, all our dreams interrupted by tangled lapses and ghostly blips in the nighttime currents.

As I approached the diner, I saw the white trailer behind me reflected in the windows. The doorway of the cab was empty, and the boys nowhere to be seen.

IV

RIGHT PLACE AT THE RIGHT TIME—EXACTLY

The road to theatrical success is strewn with blizzards, floods, typhoons, train wrecks, bad advertising, expensive travel, cold dressing rooms, dirty theaters, abuse from friends and home, complicated train schedules, broken contracts, revolutions, lost baggage, wash basins without plugs, dirty mirrors, 11 o'clock closings, 'no smoking' signs, arrogant managers.

—DANTE'S *TRUNK BOOK* FROM THE 1930S

20

CREDO

After we told the principal, the manager, the drama coach, and the student, that know one was going to stay up their, and watch us, backstage, to see just to see, for fun, through the show, the stage manager tells that kid to sneak up their to watch us. Make sure we don't drill five foot holes in his floor.

Helen and young Katy

A MAGICIAN'S ASSISTANT MUST never falter or dally. She must be organized and lovely and certainly agreeable as her body parts are switched. When she reappears out of smoke or air, she is always whole and smiling, her reliability steadfast. She will always be there after disaster, like ashes, salt, and the ground. A magician's assistant must know her own worth because no one will ever tell her.

She and the magician are partners in crime even though onstage no one suspects her complicity. The magician is an obvious target of suspicion. The very nature of his profession triggers defenses. He claims space in the collective unconscious along with the trickster, the shaman, and the temple priest. Anyone can conjure up images of the magician offstage. He is floating a matchbook in a tavern or frolicking with his magic friends—they levitate and saw each other in half at Hollywood parties. Then what of the assistant? Who is she? And what is she really thinking? In professional magic the magician's assistant is perhaps the biggest mystery.

My mother was from the old school—she played it straight. No inane beauty-queen smile touched her lips. Long ago, she found a smile that suited her. A slight serene smile, a shapely slender thing without teeth. No dint of fuss or trouble touched that smile despite the secret loads, gimmicked trays, and double-bottom boxes she carried. It conveyed a certain sincerity. It was a smile that said, *there's nothing wrong here, nothing at all.* My stage smile was too hungry, too eager. It said, *please like me.* I smiled so big and so constantly that when I walked offstage, my mouth ached.

My mother and I always posed onstage with feet together, one leg bent and arms behind us. We stood a little behind Dad to the left, or a little behind Dad to the right. We knew the score. He was helpless without us. We delivered him coins, cards, hats, bucket, powder puff, bag, and lemon. We retrieved from him silks, doves, top hat, clocks, pipe, bike locks, and cages of foam birds. I always handed him his coin bucket for the second act after the curtain closed while he was bowing on the front step. And my mother always retrieved the bucket at the end. He wouldn't even turn around. He'd just throw it behind him, because he knew, without fail, she was standing there ready to catch it. We had to be at the right place at the right time—exactly. Or all would have been lost. Without us, he would be throwing back the lids of big boxes and discovering no one there, or holding a man's watch wondering where his hammer was or just standing in the spotlight, perplexed he had finally been rendered average—just another unspectacular man with loose change in his pockets. No magic would happen, no magic at all.

After Dad's diatribe with the boys, Mom ensured he got more rest. Those long afternoon hours before the show became his quiet time. While he sat behind his trunk fiddling with his props, Mom was his vigilant sentinel.

If a stranger happened backstage, Mom intercepted him before he even reached Dad's trunk. "Can I help you?" she'd ask. All afternoon, Dad would tinker with his props, adjusting, mending, and repairing. He soaped cards, filed coins, or restitched loose snaps on the dove bags.

Whatever he needed we fetched for him. Sometimes glue, aspirin, or nail clippers.

"Do you have scissors?" he would ask, and Mom found a pair in her hobo luggage. "Do you have tissue?" and I would pluck one from Mom's tissue box.

On these afternoons, I would sit in a chair between Mom's table and Dad's trunk, a family arrangement we clung to. Without a real home on the road, we had to scrape one together on our various stages as a way of reclaiming some of the stability we'd lost. We carried three chairs—cold metal, fold-out, spray-painted matte black—which substituted for our personal household furniture.

Day to day, we assessed Dad's mood behind his trunk. On bad days, he kept his pink face down with a soldier's care to avoid artillery fire. On good days, he coasted on cool discernment through conflict. Most of the time he operated on a flat neutral, somewhere between grace and affliction. If he was tired, he would wad up his denim jacket for a pillow and head for his crude bed, the piano chair's empty crate. It opened flush to the floor, which afforded him easy access and comfortable width. He would crawl inside, a fatigued pilgrim, with half his legs sticking out. If a crew member had to step over him, he would say from inside the box, "Don't mind me," which always elicited smiles. Mom started buying cereal and would fix a bowl for him at her table, slicing a banana on top. We were so tired of restaurant food by then that a meal prepared by Mom from picnic supplies overjoyed us. Dad would slurp down the cereal and then drink the remaining milk from the carton in slow, savoring sips.

My mother had probably been caring for my father this way on the road for years. Our unpredictable helpers intensified the tension, prompting her to step up her game as protector, buffer, troubleshooter. As fortunate as my father was to have my mother's care, these roles could be dicey for her. That was probably why she was so reluctant to return to the road in the first place.

One afternoon backstage, a theater manager asked to see the insurance papers for The Floating Piano. When Mom obliged, Dad erupted. "He's harassing us!" he charged, his face pinched crimson. We were playing in a swanky stage at a new junior college, and maybe, just a little, he was right. Magic shows rank quite low in the hierarchy of theater, and the staff might have been horrified by the whiff of horse manure out the stage door, dove seeds on their polished pine floor, our thin black-velour curtains hanging on their new sleek battens, and our shabby road-worn crates next to their stage flats for *King Lear*.

To Dad's accusation Mom contended, "What else was I going to do?" and marched away to take out her frustration on a loaf of Wonder Bread.

Each night she had to prepare the bread for The Watch, a task that required her to tear out a hole in each slice, stick a light bulb in the center of the loaf, and reassemble it. On this afternoon she did a frenzied surgery with contained fury, peeling back the wrapper, ripping out the holes, sticking in the light bulb, and putting the loaf back together with fast, angry fingers. She returned it to its bag and tied a perky knot. (Onstage Dad would remove the light bulb from the loaf, tap it with a trick mallet, and a man's borrowed watch would fall out from the mallet. However, to the audience, it appeared to come from inside the light bulb that had been in a loaf of bread.) She quickly stuffed the leftover bread pieces into a grocery bag, then stuffed that bag in another bag, stuffed in another bag, stuffed in another bag, as if the heart of the loaf was insufferable in her hands. After dumping the whole thing in a backstage trash can, she stopped and wiped her hands, her face smooth and untroubled.

I looked over at the caged doves. Mom tended the Wonder Bread, and I tended the doves. Time to trim the dove wings, my most disliked task in the show. I had procrastinated for so long that the doves were gaining distance. Lately, when Dad produced them onstage, they fluttered out of his grasp, and he had to chase them. I studied the doves lined up on their perch. I reached inside the cage. The birds had been trained as babies to step on an index finger. Getting one out was easy. Then I grabbed it across its back. It pecked at my hand, fast. *Peck, peck, peck.*

That's why I hated handling the doves. Their beaks hurt, and they always agonized in my grasp. I carefully spread its delicate wing. Opening the scissors, I cut the tips of its flight feathers. I was a very good showgirl, committed to our cause, and I didn't want our birds escaping into a theater's rigging system or gym rafters or anywhere they shouldn't be, possibly missing a cue. They had to be at the right place at the right time—exactly. Their reliability steadfast.

I put away that dove and took out another. I did five more, swiftly moving through the cage, suffering through the pecks, deeply confused by my relationship with such pretty creatures, hating it all.

When I finished, the newspaper below me was covered with fragments of bird wing, feathers and shafts, soft downy fluff. I folded the newspaper and stuffed it in a bag and stuffed that in another bag, then in another bag, and another.

21

ROLLICKING REBOUND

I don't no, maybe i'am mad at the
3 of them because i'am jelouse because i'am
not good friends with them.

Katy's big moment jumping out of the top hat

HANK THE MAGICIAN WRECKED our turnout in Spokane. He
had played there a month earlier and his show was so bad nobody
wanted to buy another ticket to a magic show. Only thirty folks
showed up to our show.

At the end of the night, the sponsors asked for the pallet box used
in The Escape Box. Dad never returned the box because of the muti-
lated lid and he pretended he didn't know its whereabouts. Touching
his chest, he surveyed backstage. "Hmm, fellas, I just don't know
where it could be." That's when Hank the Magician's worst misdeed
was revealed to us. The men laughed when they told us Hank the
Magician had also done The Escape Box and left behind the rigged lid
for all to see.

"He didn't even hide it," Dad growled as we drove away that night. The tour stopped at the Idaho border.

Sponsors had sold so few tickets in Moscow, Coeur d'Alene, Idaho Falls, Twin Falls, and Pocatello that those shows were canceled.

The next morning, we pecked at our eggs in a diner in Pullman. Nine days ahead of us without a show. The boys scratched their necks lazily while Clair gazed pensively into her cup of tea.

"We might as well go to Boise," Dad declared, scraping up the last of his runny eggs. We had a show there on April 18th.

All the way south to Boise, I imagined theater after theater with mangled escape-box lids on display. Dad wanted to scratch the trick in the Boise show. "It's ruined now," he complained.

As soon as we got to the Boise motel, we retreated into our creature caves, hiding and sleeping, leaving Do Not Disturb signs on our doors all day and raiding the vending machine late at night.

At a laundromat, Mom and I washed our clothes with Clair. She sat on the folding table with her legs crossed, reading a book. I removed a novel from my tote bag and laid it on my lap. I never read a textbook in front of Clair because I didn't want to remind her or me that our original relationship was supposed to be that of teacher and student. I was surprised by my disappointment that that would not be. Left to my own schooling, algebra had become a guessing game, and I believed it was too late to ask for her help.

Clair's washed clothes were neatly stacked, her white cotton underthings modestly tucked between her shirts and jeans. She wore a maroon blouse with frilly sleeves, and her socks were spotted with perky little daisies. Ever since my rebuff of her teaching efforts, I had tried to make amends with innocuous small talk.

I folded clothes and tried again. "That color looks good on you," I said, keeping my voice cheerful.

"Thanks." Her eyes remained glued to her book. "You need more quarters?"

"I'm fine."

As she turned a page and said no more, I felt a new sting of rejection. She was riding on a river of words away from us. I vowed to give it back to her. Opening my book, I read with a stubborn focus. We bared the hard, impervious faces of our books at each other.

When Mom and I returned to the motel room, Dad was talking to Mr. Bly on the phone, with his worn briefcase open on the bed. When he hung up, he tossed his pen down on his yellow list. "I'll have to do The Escape Box." The Boise sponsors could not cancel the trick as they had already advertised it.

Our truck was parked behind the motel. Eyeing it out the window, it reminded me of a big white slumbering rabbit. The magic show had been breaking even until this ten-day layover. Now it was a losing financial venture. Dad sat on the bed with his strong, pale hands resting on his thighs to stop himself from jumping up.

"We're just collecting bills here," he said tightly.

Sleep still eluded him. He was fidgety, restless, unable to focus on the newspaper we brought him. One day, Mom and I went shopping so he could nap. When we returned, he lay in the dim room wrapped like a corpse in a white sheet.

Mom set down her purse and asked with concern, "Did you get any sleep?"

"Just rest," he said heavily.

Then one night, as dusk filled the motel windows, the Pocus Posse became antsy. We fled the quagmire of our rooms and gathered in the motel lobby with collars turned out, hair brushed, necks perfumed, and wallets full of cash. We entered, en masse, a restaurant next door, claimed a corner of the bar and pushed together the little round cocktail tables into one. Appetizers were ordered and Mom gave me quarters for the jukebox.

Dot told us she might take off for a short gambling trip to the Nevada state line. "McDermitt, Nevada—only 182 miles away," she brightly announced, mimicking the pull of a slot machine handle.

Clair removed from her purse her trusty AAA travel book and suggested Winnemucca instead. "Three-star motel, free coffee in the lobby."

Al had searched for other magicians in the Boise phone book and had found a bartender across town who did bar magic. "Holy Houdini!" He grabbed his head in anguish. "Not the coin in the beer bottle again!"

From the empty appetizer plates, Ben collected lettuce garnishes for the geese and leftover, nibbled, sparerib bones for a stray dog he had befriended. Brody called him a "pathetic wimp!" while he front- and back-palmed cards.

Suddenly Dad lurched forward in alarm. "Is that …?" He thought he saw Hank the Magician sitting at the long oak bar. We turned to search the row of stout Idahoans drinking beer with no inkling as to what the infamous magician looked like.

Al turned back and threw his napkin at Dad. "Right," he scoffed. "He's following you around. Relax, Lee."

Then Dad turned to me and pointed an accusing finger. "And you! You're no better! My best card trick!" Even as we laughed, I wondered why he kept recalling my disloyal deed. A question sparked in his eyes, a question that had not been there before.

In Boise, the sponsors delivered Dad the escape box. A dark oil drum with a flywheel on top. A nasty old thing, rusty and industrial ugly and looking as impossible to get into as it was to break out of. It was a big joke to the sponsors.

"You're not going to fool us like that other magician," they hackled.

Hank the Magician had damaged the trick again. "You've outsmarted me for sure, fellas," Dad said, grinning and shaking their hands before they left.

Our trio stared at the old oil drum. No way Dad could get out of that frightful container. Mom held her hand over her throat, too stricken to speak.

Brody and Ben joined us, shaking their heads. "That's impossible," Brody said just as Al and Dot came by.

"They're trying to kill, I mean, trick you again," Al said.

"What are you going to do now, Mr. Wonderful?" Dot said.

Dad didn't say anything.

Clair paused on her way out the stage door for her afternoon excursion.

"Lee has to escape that!" Mom exclaimed.

Clair cocked her head at the drum and sighed at this junior high prank. "You'll need air holes," she advised before continuing on her way. She was right. He could die in there.

"I gotta lie down," Dad said. He plodded off to his reclining crate.

"Lee!" Mom stomped one high heel on the floor. "What are you going to do?"

"I have a plan." He crawled inside.

To get himself out of this jam, he recruited a husky boy-mover who had helped us earlier in the day. Al scouted him out in the audience before the show and brought him to Dad, where they conferred deep in the offstage shadows next to the odious oil drum. I caught a glimpse of him, thick torso, hefty arms, a quick smile that told me he liked being taken into a magician's confidence.

As he was leaving, Dad told him, "Remember. In and out. Without ruffling the curtain."

During the show, just before The Escape Box, the kid showed up backstage, his white sneakers glowing in the dark, and Al parked him behind the slit of the backdrop. The stunt unfolded seamlessly. When Dad was in the oil drum and surrounded by the tent, the kid slipped through the backdrop and tent, which was so far upstage it abutted the curtain and the audience could not see him. Once inside, he removed the heavy lid to the oil drum for Dad to climb out.

Then Dad ran. He ran through the backdrop and stage door, and out into the night under flabbergasted stars, all the way around to the front of the theater.

From the stage, I watched him enter behind the audience, and then pace back and forth, tapping his pockets, until the time came for him to call out.

"You didn't think I could do it, did you?"

All heads turned. Within the applause I heard a few incredulous "Ohhhs." Dad's march back to the stage was victorious. After the show the sponsors inspected the oil drum for fissures, blow-torch blisters, and blasted metal.

At a diner that night, Dad exclaimed, "Did you see the looks on their faces?" He punched the air. "Let's hire that kid!"

We laughed hard and loud, so consumed by our hysterics that we could barely hold our forks. I sipped my mug of hot cocoa, relieved to be trouping again, back to these clamorous late-night meals. Even so, Dad's clever triumph had only elevated his spirits a bit, and soon he was outside our laughter, busy with his own thoughts as he chewed his bacon and buttered his toast. We had another three days before our next show in Auburn, another three days without show revenue for daily expenses— a shameful failure of numbers for my father, the businessman. He measured success in professional magic by one's ability to earn a living from it. And the show's low profits hinted that maybe, just maybe, he was falling short of his highest ideals about what it meant to be a successful magician.

He pushed away his plate and flagged the waitress for a check.

"You kids keep on going to Auburn," he announced to the table. "We're going to Lake Tahoe."

My parents had previously discussed using these free days to see Doug Henning's show at Harrah's casino in Lake Tahoe, but Dad had decided against it. Now he changed his mind.

"It'll give Henning a thrill to meet me."

Even with his crooked smile and wink, there was a moment when I completely believed him.

The next morning, we caravanned out of Idaho, cut through a corner of Oregon, and dropped down into Nevada on a ribbon of remote gray road, then turned west. At Reno, we parted. The crew headed to Auburn to wait for our next show, and our trio turned south to the

Nevada side of Lake Tahoe.

That night we sashayed into a theater loaded with cocktail wait-resses in short skirts and running waiters. Hundreds of people, packed into long tables, were swirling complimentary cocktails. We ordered dinner and gazed at the big, elegant red curtain with gathered fes-toons. It was such a large stage. It would be a long trek just to hand Dad his coin bucket. I closed my eyes, beset by equal parts fear and joy.

In his show, Doug Henning floated a golden ball, restored a burnt ribbon, and escaped from a chained box. When he sawed a woman in half, he dashed between her body parts with a skip and a hop. He still had that long hippie hair, the same moon and stars on his velvet overalls. Countless wonderments happened with a leap and a grin.

After the show, Dad removed a piece of paper from his breast pocket, jotted a note, and, as we were leaving the theater, slapped it in the hand of a waiter along with a twenty-dollar bill. "Give this to Mr. Henning!" he said and charged through the crowd. We followed him out the theater, through the casino, and onto the street.

"Where are we going, Lee?" Mom asked.

"To the Golden Pine," he said. We had seen an ad. A magician's convention was in town. Uh-oh. He was fishing for autographs!

"We're not registered," Mom said.

"I'll tell them who I am," he said and bolted ahead.

We followed him down Lake Tahoe Boulevard and into another casino, past the slot machines to the conference rooms in the back. By the door, a sign read Welcome to the United Alliance of Magicians! We walked into a huge room filled with men milling about with name tags stuck to their shirts. These magicians were identical to the Magic Gal magicians—totally unremarkable. And hordes of them. Old, dumpy, forgettable men clutching conference programs. Nobody very interesting, let alone magical, and I wondered if magic was some-thing that couldn't be seen.

With the mettle of ballsy party crashers, we passed the registration table and strolled by booths of vendors selling their magic wares. There were coin gimmicks, Svengali decks, resplendent colorful silks, billiard balls, aerial suspensions, and gold hoops of every size. I kept looking into the crowd for an onrush of Dad's exuberant fans. We situated ourselves in the center of the huge room for optimal visibility and gazed down at the commercial-grade carpet and up to the high, airy rafters. It occurred to me that we were supposed to wait without giving the appearance of waiting. We made small talk. "How was that chicken piccata?" "Isn't that a flying bird cage over there?" I fidgeted, twirling locks of hair and tugging my earlobe. The truth was clear: No one remembered America's Leading Magician of the 1950s. Maybe Mom had the same thought. We both scanned the crowd for a Magic Gal magician, or any familiar face, while Dad kept his chin high, an obstinate spark in his eye. Then I had a startling thought. Maybe Dad never was America's Leading Magician of the 1950s. That title reeked of sophisticated hokum.

Mom's nothing-wrong-here smile was in full force. "Let's play the nickel machines," she encouraged.

He looked away, pretending he didn't hear.

I wordlessly stared into the sea of roving magicians and wondered why we were even here. Our trio had been having a fun night (*You're a card! I'm going to turn you into a rabbit!*). Now we were on this embarrassing expedition. I have since come to understand we were not enough for my father. My mother gave him a home and family. She baked him beautiful lemon meringue pies, bought him new ties, socks and boxers. Still, what he yearned for was beyond what she, or any of us, could give him. To love a great magician is to live in astonishment and to endure.

A man approached us with an official badge pinned to his teal jacket. He looked us over for registration tags. Busted! He was going to ask us to leave! My heart stopped.

Pointing a finger at Dad, he said, "I think I've seen you." His eyebrows knitted together. "You're ...?"

Dad stuck out his hand. "I'm Lee Grabel. We happened to be in the area and wanted to drop by."

He was Bob from Grass Valley. Mom and I loved Bob from Grass Valley and showered him with big, grateful smiles. He'd seen the show as a little boy in El Paso. Bob was followed by Glen and Rudy, long-ago fans from Texarkana and Fargo. Somewhere in the flurry of excitement, my doubt vanished faster than a lady in a box.

I saw two ungainly teenage boys with oily faces ogle Dad from the sidelines. I heard one say, "I thought he was dead." My father had been absent so long from professional magic, his death was easy to assume.

We left Lake Tahoe the next day in good spirits, as if we'd coast through the rest of the tour on luck and good humor. All that changed once we left the pine-scented mountains. Thrust into the byways and streets of more towns that weren't home, the mood in the car shifted. The weight of our problematic tour, with the Napa filming in nine days, filled us with a sense of unease. When we pulled up to the theater in Auburn, we were silent.

That night Ben and Brody forgot to place the portable center steps from the stage to the front row seats. This forced Dad to use the stage right steps. Each time he needed a volunteer, he had to walk all the way over and back, which slowed the pace of the show and tired him. And that night, we had a mild catastrophe in our Roseville motel room. The heating and cooling system had been installed in reverse, which meant when we turned on the heat the air conditioning came on. The colder we got, the higher Dad turned up the chill. When he figured it out, it was daylight, and all chance of decent slumber gone.

That afternoon, on a stage smelling of soda and popcorn, I packed the top hat with its foulards and foam birds, feeling Dad behind me, brooding and fretting at his wardrobe trunk. The filming of the Napa show was one week away, and I didn't know if we could pull off a good show, not with the crew still prone to error and with Dad's foul mood. We needed fabulous footage to attract Vegas venues. My parents had also broken their usual reserve and invited their Alamo business friends. This added a new layer of pressure for me and probably my parents, too.

I finished the top hat and then moved on to my other duties. The entire crew was preparing the show for that night. We were quiet as we shuffled around with heads down, winding up equipment like flimsy timepieces.

22

EXTRAORDINARY MISHAPS
FOR ORDINARY PEOPLE

The Nappa show didn't go to good. But it
wasn't our fault. All the things that happened was the
equipments problems.

The Floating Lady

THE NEXT DAY, MOM and I watched Dot set up her concession
stand at a big high school gym in Sacramento.

"Those boys just aren't helping Al," Dot said, slamming down a
six-pack of cola on her table. "Al had to unload that piano by himself!
Brody walked right on by without helping!" She sounded piston-pop-
ping angry. "And you know what Clair told me? Those boys call Al
old!"

Our jaws dropped. No one pushing sixty was old! Some people pushing sixty took their magic shows back on the road!

"And Helene"—her voice dropped— "Al's shoehorn is missing."

Mom was about to speak until Dot made the "stop" gesture. "He won't say anything to those boys. He's too proud."

There was more. Dot said Al told the cousins to be ready at ten this morning. "Damn if those boys were still sleeping when we got there. So I said to Brody, 'Don't you care about this magic show?' And he says, 'Why should I? No one sees it anyway.'"

She stacked soda cans in a pyramid. "You know, Al might not come back 'cause of those boys."

Mom gulped. "We can't do it without Al."

Dot put the last can on top of the pyramid and admired her work. "I could make good money tonight."

She removed from her purse four thin paperback books and handed them to me. "I thought you might want these since you read a lot." On the covers were women in skimpy negligees sitting on the ground looking up at men with guns. Some of the women appeared afraid of the men with guns, and others seemed to like the men with guns.

As Mom and I walked down the aisle toward the stage, she grabbed them from my hands. "I can't believe she gave you those!"

I felt my bra strap pressing into my skin. It bound my breasts so tight it left lines on my shoulder. That's how puberty sometimes felt, excruciatingly uncomfortable. I wasn't me anymore. I didn't know who I was, and no one else did either.

I followed Mom backstage, relieved she'd yanked those books away. They frightened me, and I didn't want to hurt Dot's feelings by not reading them. I watched Mom throw them away, stuffing them in a grocery bag, then in another bag, and then burying them deep in a trash can in the corner.

I slipped out the stage door to walk around the theater, then stopped. I didn't want to bump into Clair on her afternoon roaming. I headed for the Cadillac and sat there, consumed by Brody's words. *No one sees it anyway.* I've come to understand Brody was a typical nineteen-year-old, fueled by angst and rebelling against instruction. Back then, though, he felt mysteriously hostile. I still stewed over his "ugly" remark. At first, I had expected Brody to shuffle up one day and mumble an apology, only to realize, as the towns racked up, that this would never happen. It was the first time I ever hated another person.

From the car window, I watched Brody stride out the stage door and disappear behind the truck. I thought about the casino talent scouts. Just one dumb, careless act by the boys would ruin the Vegas show. Because of them the show might never play again. This felt unbearable to me. In the most unlikely places, I had found magic. The open road after midnight, the throbbing light of the stage, the dreary dressing rooms and vanities with missing light bulbs that cast me in a flattering Floridian tan. I was so angry at Brody for not understanding it, for having the power to take that away, that my heart clenched in a fist. I had a nice-girl fit right in the car. "*Brody!*" I cried and flung a book against the dashboard.

During the show that night, Brody darted over to Mom's table stage right.

"We can't do it, the string broke," he said.

The string for The Floating Lady. It had broken again when he was preparing the trick for the next number. Behind the closed curtain, the stepladder was in the middle of the stage under an arrangement of black fish line. Brody trotted away and Mom grabbed a hammer. Dad needed it onstage to crush a man's watch.

I waited at Mom's table in my floating lady costume, looking at the show's lineup. We would have to replace The Floating Ball and The Floating Lady with The Substitution Trunk. Behind her nothing-wrong-here smile, Mom was just then breaking the news to Dad onstage. She tossed back the curtain and rushed to her table.

"He wants Brody to fix it and we'll do it anyway," she said breathlessly. "Go tell him."

I rushed off and found Brody stage left. He was pulling up his black socks, balancing on one shiny black shoe at a time.

I was happy to be giving him the news. "Dad wants to do the trick anyway," I snapped.

He was ready for combat. "He can't do that!" he barked, his eyes flashing and mouth tight.

"You don't have a lot of time," I warned him.

From the wings, I watched Brody quickly rethread the entire routine, stepping up and down the ladder and running the string between his fingers. He then rolled out the levitation table. Not much time was left before the curtain opened.

During the routine, when Brody came onstage to retrieve the ball, Dad turned off the microphone around his neck. I didn't hear his exact words because of the music, but it was clear he was chewing Brody out as he delicately maneuvered the ball back into its silken box.

I stood in the wings, coldly watching, rejoicing in my father's verbal lashing. Brody moved stiffly onstage, his face expressionless. When my part came for The Floating Lady, I walked onstage and stood before Dad, who wiggled his fingers in a mock hypnotic dance. I fell backward into Brody's hands. His touch felt heavy, his fingers dragged by a torrent. On the table, I fluttered my closed eyelids and glimpsed Brody's squeezed face in the spooky, watery light. Soon, I was encased in the table and rolling off the stage.

The levitation worked fine that night. The wire lady didn't rise crooked or drop to the floor with a thud. Brody had restrung the arrangement quickly and correctly. It was a meager blessing. My father's anger legitimized my own, and at the end of the night I watched Brody haul crates, my eyes squinty with anger.

When the show was packed, I stood at the stage door, looking out at the parking lot. Brody stood in the cold night air watching the idling truck, his hands on his hips and his loose russet hair curling around his ears. My anger was alive, streaming through my body, a dark rushing river. I couldn't stop myself. I walked toward him. Then stopped. Started again. I stood next to him. The truck's taillights cast us both in a crimson hue. He turned to me, half his face lit in scarlet. A small shadow touched that soft spot above his lip, a broken invitation. I blamed him for everything. Every blunder and near-blunder, lost money and lost sleep, capped off by the geese fiasco. And sweet Al, stuck stage left with him. What hurt most was his rejection of me. My anger gathered into smoke and grit and formed into words.

"You're making Al do all the work!" I snapped. My nerves triggered Katy Gwabel, and I mispronounced "work" so that it sounded like "wawk."

Brody didn't notice. Halfway through, my anger fizzled right out of me, and I had a nineteen-year-old boy glaring at me in the fiery red truck lights. He hadn't understood a single word I had said, only that he was being blamed for something. He screwed up his face. "What?"

I repeated it flatly, prefacing it with, "Dot said," this time crushingly timid, careful in my pronunciation, feeling cursed before I was even done. "Dot says you're making Al do all the work," I squeaked.

Brody's body erupted, his face alive with fury as he snarled, "You tell Dot to mind her own business!" He stalked off.

My hands shook. I tucked them under my armpits and walked away, my heart pounding.

We got closer to Napa—five, four, three days away. We played another high school gym and a funky lecture hall in a junior college. Behind us, we left lipstick marks on coffee mugs and old pantyhose stuffed into dressing room trash cans. On every stage floor, we left random cards dropped from Dad's manipulation routine, orphaned jacks, fives, and deuces for the janitor. Mostly, we left miles of scrolling white lines behind us as we barreled down the road.

I had discovered the road was the same everywhere. The waitresses, motel clerks, and boy-movers didn't change as much as became interchangeable. Maybe all of us were interchangeable, too. The magic show was the vessel for everyone's deepest desires, and we passed through as believers or not. Sometimes late at night, I buried my nose in my arm. That smell. The smell of the magic show. My skin was infused with its ripe, fleshy imprint.

One night during intermission, I saw something on my Dad's thumb. He was standing in the wings about to walk out for the second half, his gold medal catching scant light and alabaster hair glowing against the black curtain. Reaching into his pocket, he removed a horrid little gizmo. A fake flesh-colored plastic thumb-tip with a razor blade crudely duct-taped to the top. He scratched the air with it, then put it in his pocket. My eyes narrowed. What was that for? *Oh, I know.* That was how he cut the strings of the wire lady.

Back in a motel bathroom that night, I recorded my findings in my red journal. I also wrote about silks on a string, eyelets on a silver ball, the mallet head with the secret compartment, and the big silver ring with the gap in it. I knew it was wrong. I was still that fourth grader who revealed Dad's card trick. I can see now that I was really a tourist in my father's magic show, soaking up ambiance and taking notes. As we get older, it is not the things we will never do that are hard to accept, it is that we are not the people we hoped we would be.

I closed my journal and studied the cover, worn by use and travel. The edges of the pages were ruffled and smudged with face makeup. A Chiquita Banana sticker dotted the front, and densely layered doodle-work was inked on the back. The journal wasn't just bound paper anymore. It was a living, growing article of my creation. My little purple notebook was filling up, as well, with Pocus Posse chatter in my big loopy letters, some of it swollen by table water and flecked with dry egg.

Dad assumed all this writing was for the article, yet week after week, I showed him nothing. In a diner, the night before the Napa show, as I removed the notebook from my purse, Dad asked, "How's that article coming?" By then I had abandoned the notion I would ever write it and opted for the same subterfuge he had used with my grandparents.

"Don't worry," I said too quickly. "I got it. Almost done."

Suddenly, his arm flew out toward my notebook. I pulled back before he snatched it away. He smiled playfully but I knew his curiosity was piqued. He had finally figured out that I wasn't working on the article. Then what, he must have asked himself, is she writing? If I hadn't exposed his card trick in the fourth grade, he might have deemed my scribbling harmless. Instead, it made me more suspicious to him. If he had asked me what the notetaking was for, I truly could not have told him. I just knew something important was happening to me, and I wanted to write it down.

Al must have sensed Dad's concern over that little purple notebook. He poured cream into his coffee and remarked, "She's a spy for Blackstone. Relax, Lee."

Dad brandished a digit at him. "Hey, can you work with a sore thumb?" He studied me over the rim of his coffee cup.

I moved my notebook protectively to my purse. My notetaking now felt tainted by wrongdoing. To this day, I don't think it was the secrets of the stage my father feared I was recording. It was my innocent musings in my girlish felt pens that concerned him. Maybe he sensed I had seen something in his character, something even he didn't want to see.

After that, I was careful. At our diner meals, I held the notebook close to my chest in case I got ambushed. I didn't feel so invisible or inconsequential anymore. My mistakes were catching up to me. The unrepairable chasm between Clair and me had taken its toll. Worse yet was my outburst with Brody. Whenever he passed me, he would look away and tighten his jaw. It wasn't just me. He was in retreat from all of us. He never lingered stage right; he passed through with the speed of a person fleeing a crime. In his wake, he left the smoke of his motion and the *clack* of his patent leather shoes.

And if Dad asked him a question, he gave a fast answer and made a faster exit. In his pockets, Brody had replaced those wily court cards with hard, salty corn nuts. In his free time, he flipped through sports magazines, and I soon picked up snatches of talk drifting through various dreary afternoon stages. When the tour ended, he told Ben, he would sell car tires, patch potholes, or wash dishes, save money and take off to scale famous glacial peaks or canoe down wild rivers or journey deep into the wilderness with only a hatchet and a handful of salt. "Once this stupid magic show is over."

In The Backstage, each time I entered the box, I sensed him close by, stooping in the dark with the poise of a cat burglar. I nearly expected his hand to pop out to pinch me. All that empty secret space became imbued with danger. Curled up inside the trap, I kept my hand in a fist over my mouth to hold back, too late, my damning words. Even The Floating Lady felt tinged with threat. That moment I tipped back felt endless. Falling, falling...I was unsure if he would be there to catch me. Then, finally, his cool hands on my back.

Filming anything in 1977 required lots of space and techies. A film crew arrived before the Napa show, carting in bulky equipment and claiming a block of seats in the center of the auditorium. I accompanied Dad to inspect the setup. On a stand, they had erected a camera with a protruding lens and a grim elongated body in glintless black. Just seeing it pointed at the stage made my heart plunge. It was as if a large, unwelcome insect had flown in on the winds of rumor and ruin. A thin, square-faced photographer showed up. Around his neck on a big strap hung a camera with a huge telephoto lens and a teetering skyscraper flash. He told us he would be moving fast in The Opening, up and down the foot of the stage "catching the action," and we should ignore the light when the flashes went off.

Committing the show to celluloid had a high-stakes finality to it. Backstage I roamed, constantly checking my makeup and tugging at my nylons, inconsolably nervous. I was convinced the film would enter an old stone fortress of magician archives and be the definitive record of our magic show for eternity.

Fortunately, we had a proper stage at Napa High School. Another of the many modest working stages we had grown accustomed to, with blotched pine floors, worn curtains, and dressing rooms with old, laminated counters. We had a good turnout, over three hundred. Through the curtain, I could see the lively contingent from Alamo. Dad's golf foursome and their wives, salesladies from the office, and various business associates chatting across the seats.

Before the show, at Dad's bidding, the crew assembled for a talk stage right with the exception of Brody, whom Al had to flag down and escort over to our group. We stood in a circle, gazing at Dad's greased face and newly barbered silver hair. With his silky black tails and gold medal around his neck, he could have doubled as a decorated diplomat on his way to a gala affair. He explained the importance of recording a good show tonight and launched into a medley of stage tips and reminders: "Keep the pace. Be ready for your cues. Look sharp." I glanced at Brody gazing down at the floor. Dad ended with, "Let's do it," and I followed him with an enthusiastic "Yeah!" My exclamation was negated by the empty space the crew left in its wake as they quickly dispersed into the shadows.

When I wonder why my father wanted to be a magician, I sometimes examine his old manipulation deck I keep in my desk drawer. I study the storied suits, speculating on their allures and temptations. Perhaps it was the mighty king of spades, the most darkly arresting, who seduced my father, or the king of diamonds, for the fortune it implied. Or all the handsome bachelor aces. Maybe it was romantic images of riverboat gamblers and worldly men in dark suits and the grand Howard Thurston, the leading magician of his youth, who flung cards with precision to folks in the audience. His London crowds would call out to him, "Throw cards! Throw cards!" I now believe we can't understand our passions or the mysterious journey on which they take us. And to ask any magician why is to hear only of the intangibles. Energy in motion, nameless onrushing forces, a yearning that never sleeps.

What I do know is that my father didn't believe in magic. He believed in empirical evidence, and if it could not be touched, smelled, tasted, heard, or seen, it didn't exist. Magicians who touted the supernatural annoyed him. Such claims were just an extension of the onstage act to him. No wands, no magic words, no easy wins. *Nothing happens unless you make it happen* was his testament to being responsible for your dreams. He wasn't afraid of toiling for what he wanted, as is evident in both his careers. A real estate agent when no one was buying, and a traveling showman when the road was dead.

In the coming years, I would meet no one like him. All his fortitude and worldly powers would be unmatched by the men I would love. Men without unusual preoccupations. Men who were lonely, sad, young, and old, exhausted men who couldn't spell or drive a car or hold down a job; men with an injury of spirit or body, men without hope. Still, they would give me the sweetness my father never did, yet fail to give me what I most loved about him—his ability to create something out of nothing.

My father has always been my best story, my steward and crusader against the commonplace. Just by being his daughter, I have always been a special citizen of the world. When my nights are crowded by my failures, I imagine him nose down and vision straight, donning his black coattails and polishing his shoes, even as defeat knocks on his dressing room door, whether it be muscle spasm in his hands, mutinous help, a heckler in the back row, or flames engulfing the theater.

Perhaps my father's biggest gift to me was not his love, time, or effort, but showing me his magic show. There was something in the magic show's bloated star-smacked light I will never find again. That is probably why I never threw away my red journal, and why I ponder those old photos, always pausing on the ones from the Napa show taken by that photographer. The one of me jumping out of that hat, arms raised high to catapult myself out of this stratosphere. Another of me chatting it up onstage with a volunteer, mouth unabashedly open, exposing all that Christmas tinsel.

For a long time that Napa video, on a VHS cassette, was in a bottom drawer of my parents' television cabinet. Over the years, I've watched it several times, as it's one of the only recordings of the magic show. Through the fast-moving gritty darkness, I see the wire lady's white sheath waving like a flag of surrender, and I curse the video for immortalizing all that happened that spring, as I aim the remote at the screen and pull the trigger.

In the second half of the Napa show, Brody suddenly appeared at Mom's workstation. Standing on the edge of the table light, he silently read that night's lineup, pinned to the curtain. I tried to ignore him but couldn't. He had neatly tucked in his shirt and worn his bow tie. His body was perfectly still. Only his eyes moved as he read, perhaps in an attempt to be inconspicuous. Then he sharply turned and left, just a troubling thought disappearing.

The Floating Lady went fine until the end, the crowd's murmur, a fast and swift rising tide. Behind Dad on the ground lay the exposed wire lady in the light. The white satin cover was still in his hands. He waved it once, twice, and threw it down as if dirty laundry.

Brody had pulled the wrong light switch. At that moment, the photographer quit snapping photos while the camera rolled on.

Backstage there was a commotion. From the light panel stage right, Brody said, "Damn!" Instead of the floodlights aimed directly into the audience, blinding them so they could not see the wire form, he had flipped on the footlights, which shined directly on the stage. Then he turned on the right switch too late.

The wire lady had been exposed.

"Close the drapes now! Now!" I heard Al holler. Mom frantically pulled the line. Brody threw back the curtain and emerged from the light panel, dashing past in the same fast exit he had been rehearsing for weeks. I watched him walk away, unable to speak. He kept on at a crisp clip, disappearing stage left. A dead spot opened in my brain and spread.

Years later, when I search for this incident in my journal, I will not find it. All the most painful episodes of the tour will be absent.

I wanted Dad to stop the show. Walk offstage and demand to

know from Brody what happened. I knew better. I heard his patter for the next routine. "I need to borrow a watch, a watch, please, from a man in the audience." His voice had the same blank fuzzy quality it had after the geese defecated onstage.

Mom flew to her table and cried, "Poor Lee!" and dashed onstage with her props.

I stood there for a long time, expecting Brody to come back and explain. I replayed his exclamation—*Damn!*—straining to hear horror and apology in his voice and not the scorn I thought I heard.

All this was a long time ago, and even as I write this, caution falls across the keyboard. I imagine Brody reading this and calling me, and after more than forty years, I can hear the brooding nineteen-year-old boy on the phone armed with a caustic remark, and it amazes me that in a faraway place in my thinking, he still occupies space.

At a diner that night, Dad and I sat at the far end of the table away from Brody, outside the Pocus Posse's ring of laughter. Dad leaned his elbows on the table as he waited for his eggs. I suspect beneath his stoic stance he felt powerless. We could not fire our rogue assistant. We needed him for the Vegas show eleven days away. Every now and then I glowered at Brody, which went unnoticed as he spieled off his little jokes and smirks. Either he was truly oblivious to me or intentionally ignoring the hostile vibe at the end of the table.

When we got into the car, Dad leaned heavily on the wheel again and said, "Whatdoesheknowhe'sjustalittleboy." He straightened up.

As we pulled out into the dark road, I dreaded the sabotage Brody could do at the Las Vegas show. I wondered whom Dad could trust. Who really cared about the magic show? The answer came to me in the cool, leathery air of the car. *My mother and me.* We were glamorous miners backstage in the faint light, prepared to bore through rock and impossible odds with our thin-muscled arms and industrious spunk. His best girl Fridays in our patchwork sequins and sturdy black high heels. In the car we both had our hands in our laps. I could see our reflections in the dark car glass, our figures punctured by distant light and porous to the movement of the night.

23

⁓

ILLUSIONS AND DELUSIONS

to fill you in, before i became interrupted. But i've got have to say i'm writeing a letter. and i'd

Helen, 1969

WE PLAYED A SCATTERING of towns along the Central Valley. Pulling into Bakersfield late one night, we checked into a big motel by the highway and slid into starched white sheets. The next morning we drove to the theater, passing fields of leafy green crops. Mom peered out the window. "I wonder what that is?" she mused. Dad's and my eyes skimmed over the greenery. She continued, "Collards? Chard? Mother used to cook chard in the winter."

Dad curled and uncurled his fingers on the wheel, adjusted and readjusted himself in his seat. I imagined things moving across his broad forehead, clouds shifting their shapes and shadows. His voice cut the quiet.

"We're going to start showing up at the theater at six o'clock," he announced.

Mom looked at him. "Six o'clock? We can't get there at six."

I nodded my head in silent agreement even as Dad's shoulders squared in a serious way.

"The crew can set up for us," he firmly stated.

Mom raised her eyebrows. "Sure, they can."

"Considering our stature in the business, all we have to do is show up."

"*Right, Lee,*" she said, screwing up her face.

"What do you mean?" His eyes flamed with anger. "It's a good show, the boys can handle it! We shouldn't have to babysit all day!"

"Lee!" Mom exclaimed, palms up to beseech the gods for reason. "Are you *crazy?*"

He turned the car, bouncing over potholes, into the empty parking lot of a farm and feed store. "There's nothing wrong with this magic show!" he declared. Stopping the car, he jumped out and started pacing back and forth, trapped on a tightrope, in his chocolate ankle boots.

"I'll tell you what's wrong. You said the piano was too small!" He poked his finger at Mom in the car.

"For heaven's sake!" she protested.

"You said my floating lady was sloppy!"

She gasped. "Oh, come on!"

"You said my One-Handed Card Production was piffle!"

"Get in the car!" she demanded.

He got back in, breathed deep, and dragged his hand through his bone-white hair. We drove silently out of the parking lot.

Mom closed her eyes and pinched the bridge of her nose. "I only said the lady *wobbled* when you cut the strings." She snapped up her purse. "Find a grocery store. We need bread and lemon for the show."

In the backseat, I watched the passing car lots selling pickups and recreational vehicles. Strutting in just before the show started was a wacky idea. I pressed my palm against my cheek. Dad was hunched over the wheel to stop himself from being dragged away by an invisible undertow. I have often wondered why my father chose an illusion show to appear all-powerful. An illusion show, which, by its very nature, required him to be dependent on others and, therefore, quite helpless.

"You're working yourself up into a state again." Mom crossed her arms. "Remember Illinois."

I had heard about Illinois.

In 1954, my father had been hospitalized for exhaustion in

Galesburg for two weeks, and they'd had to find another magician to replace him. *Stress management is for sissies.* He sat totally still in the car seat, his hands melded to the wheel. It had never occurred to me that the magic show could send him to the hospital. I imagined us stranded in some motel by the interstate, waiting for him to show up, twirling his Panama hat and waving his yellow list. Maybe the tour was coming undone at this very moment, diminishing into a paper cup of sequins and sparkles.

For so long I had considered Brody a hazard to the show. Now another force was loose, something internal, slithering around our trio, daring us to name it.

In recent days, Dad had become our trio's perverse outlaw, orbiting around us, never landing to even crack a smile. We could hardly avoid him, and he could not escape us or the crowds, crew, sponsors, and schedule of shows. I don't know how he performed each night, prancing, beguiling, and winking at strangers in every hamlet high and wide. He had to constantly switch personas, depending on the act, from charming gent to sly trickster to wonder-worker. Only someone who had seen the show many times would notice the heaviness of his tread and patter. An air of vacancy drifted from him, as if Lee Grabel had already played and left town a long time ago.

As we searched for a grocery store, Dad's face was closed tight as a lid, his inky blue eyes boring a hole into the traffic ahead. In the passenger seat, Mom stroked the deep lifeline running across her soft palm and scanned the storefronts out the window. She wore a fashionable blazer, big gold earrings flanking her face.

As Dad had become more withdrawn, my mother's stability had been comforting to me. I felt heartened by the grocery list she retrieved from her purse as we pulled into the store parking lot. We needed a lemon for The Lemon, Wonder Bread and a light bulb for The Watch, newspaper to change the dove cage, and pantyhose. She had a determined focus as she exited the car on her mission, with me trailing behind her. In the store, I could hardly keep up with her as she scouted the aisles.

In the checkout line, her basket was piled high with three loaves, four lemons, a bunch of nylons, and newspapers. Gazing at tabloid headlines, she started to drift inside the salacious banners. Freak spectacle, murder, and treachery—the strain of a thorny problem played across her face before subsiding into calm. She shifted her weight and brightly announced, "Mom and Dad's anniversary is this weekend. I must call."

I numbly nodded, only being polite. My life felt very distant from my friendly aunts and uncles at those big family gatherings in Oklahoma.

When we arrived at the theater, they had set up our proscenium in a gym. As I readied my props for the show, Dad barged by me, pointing and giving orders for setting up. Then he walked into a curtain batten someone had left lowered at head level. A little thunderbolt of blood bloomed across his forehead.

Mom and I administered to his wound, making him sit down while we fluttered around.

Mom handed him tissue. "Press down." I found the antibacterial ointment in the hobo luggage. As she applied the Band-Aid, his face was pink and puckered. Then he planted his Panama hat on his head and rushed off.

Mom returned to her table and the Wonder Bread. I watched her prepare it for that night's show, stooping down behind her table and tearing out the center of the loaf with a warm, soft sigh. And, with another sigh, stuffing the pieces in a bag inside a bag inside a bag.

Suddenly, Dad stood before me in military posture, chest out and shoulders back with drill-sergeant precision. "Stand straight," he sternly told me. I did that, and, nodding his head in approval, he took off. I had been slouching again. I dropped my head, feeling like I was in the crosshairs of his distress. I used Brody's same fast retreat, just a rush of steps out the stage door and to the Cadillac. Inside, the stillness of the car calmed me. I imagined my parents waiting out the long hours before showtime in the theater. My mother sitting in the chair by her table with no one to talk to; my father fussing with his props behind his trunk; and between them, my empty chair.

I got out my math book. I remembered my few short study sessions with Clair. Beneath her teacherly zeal was a gentle playfulness I never got to know. I stifled a groan. Now she hated me, and so did Brody. I felt a confusing new affinity for the cheeky young boy. For the first time I didn't know who was right or wrong. I caught my reflection in the side mirror, my empty stare and wooden mouth. My invisible crowds could not see me this way, and I reached out the window to reposition the mirror.

One person was always missing from my invisible crowds. My father. In my imagination, he was always too busy with his own big dream to sit in my audience as a fan. He learned about my success while speeding by newspaper stands, glimpsing headlines about my glorious performances far and wide. I suspect this was one reason why I had such a craving for grandeur. Because my own fame, of all things, would impress him.

That night, after we closed with The Cannon, we took curtain calls. We bowed, and the curtain closed. The curtain opened, we bowed again. Applause dropped off, and the curtain closed. We turned around to walk offstage when Dad signaled the stagehand again. The curtain opened. This time the crowd raised their eyebrows, surprised to see the seven of us, still bowing, not quite ready to leave. The curtain closed. "Okay, okay," we all said, turning away. But Dad signaled for another curtain call, and *swoosh* went the curtain across the stage. Turning around, we awkwardly bowed to the meager applause. The curtain closed and opened again. People held their sweaters and purses, gawking at us. We squirmed and withered in the light, twisted away with our uncommitted bodies while Dad bowed slow and long, oblivious to the folks leaving the theater. The spotlight's intensity gnarled his figure and blurred him at the edges; its white-hot beam had turned him into vapor.

24

EXACTLY

7th graders showed up for unloading and they couldn't lift out half the show.

The Grabels, 1979

THAT NIGHT, WE HURTLED onward past a slate-gray reservoir next to dry, craggy hills, then down a dark byway edged in orchards and punctuated by bunches of tilting mailboxes. We passed little houses drawn shut with sleep, and we kept on under a starless night sky. Up ahead, we saw a bevy of lights. Buildings emerged in a long line, and streetlights cast perfect pools of calm white light. I had this sense of dropping back down to Earth. We passed empty parking lots and crouching closed storefronts. Barbers, appliance stores, dry cleaners, shoe-repair shops, and grocery stores rolled by. Come morning those establishments would be bustling with people, and we would be tucked away on some dim stage setting up our trays, tables, and doodads until night, when the show flipped on with the snap of a finger. In the play of night and day, I belonged to the night, where I traveled by moonlight, red rouge still on my cheeks. I would never find such bounty again in daylight working hours.

The next day on a high school stage in Fillmore, I hurriedly did my preshow duties and fled to the Cadillac, where I read until near showtime. When I returned, Mom was sitting in the gummy dark by her table, fixed in her seat and still as glass. Seeing me, she moved her legs, and I could tell she had been sitting there for a long time. She got up as if from a bog of mud, and we went to the dressing room to change for the show. Nylons, sequins, high heels, a smudge of blush, face powder, and the delicate stroke of a mascara wand.

When we were done, we waited until we heard the first sound of shrieking kids running down the aisles. We did a lot of waiting on tour. As the tour carried on, the magic show with its light and music felt more unreal while waiting enveloped us. We waited for the next town, theater, motel, and diner; we waited for what would happen next.

That night, I stood by Mom at her table as Dad's jolly patter traveled to us through layers of deep artificial atmosphere. Walking offstage, my smile dropped away once I hit the wings, and I felt a surge of boredom and angst.

A local pianist banged out a tune on the pink-tinted piano that night. A spunky rendition of "You Are My Sunshine" filled the theater as the piano hit its apex and turned. Just as the pianist's body slid one way and her long hair fell away from her ear, she stopped playing. Her hands clutched her seat. Dad stopped his majestic arm undulations and leaned toward her. The theater was completely quiet.

I heard her frightened whisper. "I can't play. I didn't think it was really going to turn upside down."

Dad turned off his wireless microphone and told her, "Ma'am, you must keep playing. The music is what keeps it up." After that, she played with a newfound zest and hit the keys hard to combat the loss of gravity through the upward turn.

In a diner outside the city limits, Dad repeated his line. "Keep playing, the music is what keeps it up!" Our boundless brassy laughter sent us reeling. The pressure of the road dissipated with that laughter. We laughed like we had never laughed before, like it was all we had, like it could be our last time.

On our way out the door, Dad said to a startled diner, "Harold Flybacher! Does your wife know you're here?" and we stumbled away, too giddy to walk straight, hands over our mouths.

That night, we drove through the Mojave Desert to Ridgecrest and checked into a motel, where we drew the heavy drapes against a streetlight and fell into itchy sheets. When I woke up the next morning, my first thought was Vegas three days away. Tonight we would play the stage at a military base, the next night Barstow, then we'd make that long trek across the desert to that glitzy city. As we packed, Dad's face was expressionless. I worried he wouldn't be at his best for the casino talent scouts.

We were late and had to get to the stage for the night's show. We were about to leave when Mom checked the time. She jumped two hours ahead. It was 11:00 a.m. in Oklahoma.

"I have to call," she said, hurrying over to the phone. Her sisters would be at her parents' house to drive them to their big sixtieth wedding anniversary party at Eischen's Bar in Okarche. She talked to her sisters Kate, Ruth Ann, and Minnie Mae, who told her all the townsfolk would be there, old friends, neighbors, teachers, her best friend Juanita Lempke, and even the old town bootlegger.

She chatted happily through the entire call. When she got off, she glared at Dad. In a voice low and flat she said, *"I can't believe I'm not there."* Her features went blank. She turned away from us and curled up on the bed.

I can still recall her curved back and my young self's strong desire to bend over her and peek at her face. Instead, Dad and I stared. She looked like she had suddenly lost strength while making the bed. Crossing and uncrossing his legs, Dad squirmed in his chair, all trace of his foul mood replaced by worry.

I could see the bumps of her spine through her beige silk blouse and the scuffed bottom of her high heels. I hoped she was just sleeping. I walked to the bathroom, waited, flushed the toilet, and walked back so I could see her face. Even though her eyes were closed, I knew she was awake and trying to escape Dad, me, the tour, everything. Dad's arm lay on the little table by the window, his masonic ring and rubbery fingers silently tapping the surface, searching for the code to make her rise as simply as a wire lady on fishline. Each time he looked away, he always returned to her ruptured figure. There had to be a way to pursue a dream without taking hostages.

And what about me? I had been too focused on myself to care about the missed anniversary party. I had rejected Oklahoma, joined forces with my father to pressure her into going, and coveted her position in the magic show. My mother's toppled, curled form dwarfed the immense calling of Vegas. Dad glanced at his watch. We were going to be late to the theater. She had to get up or she'd miss her cue. Outside, the spring gusts had kicked up, battering the windows and squeezing through the panes in a long wail.

I have the gimmick my mother used to escape The Substitution Trunk, a standard trick in which an assistant, locked inside a trunk, trades places with the magician. The gimmick is a snap hook with a small corner bracket bent into a circle. While tied in a bag and locked in a trunk, these tools aided my mother's arduous escape. How this is so, I have no idea. During the trick she hid those gizmos in her cleavage. After they retired, she spray-painted the pieces gold, wore them on a chain, and eventually gave them to me.

Sometimes, I look at it when I am feeling particularly trapped by my limitations. I think of her time in confined spaces, her flying, scrambling body, and the many times she did that cannon trick over the years, matinee and evening shows, in every far-flung hamlet, for nine months each year. They always played the Marine Corps' rambunctious anthem "Stars and Stripes" with its piercing cymbal claps that resounded in a call of danger. Aiming the barrel over the heads of the audience, Dad would call out, "Good luck on your journey!"

I never could imagine her flying through billows of smoke away from us. It simply didn't fit. To me, the most likely ending had always been that she turns around midflight to cook us a big dinner in her resplendent cannon outfit. Then, at the end of the table, she entertains us with stories of fried chicken dinners for twenty and planting vegetable gardens in muddy high-heeled sandals. And more stories about living out of a suitcase nine months a year and raising a daughter on the road. Stories of levitation, transposition, startling vanishes and appearances, of being shot into the cosmos, and her regular return home.

My mother lay unmoving for about an hour. When she got up, she smoothed down her hair, checked her earrings, and opened her hands to ensure all ten nails were still red and shiny. As we headed for the theater, Mom's collapse went unmentioned. That night when she was lifted out of the box in The Cannon, she looked unspent and unruffled, her lipstick unsmudged. She and Dad clasped hands and raised them high in a victory pose and bowed. There they were, my dazzling parents, caught in a net of applause and white light. Mom was about to run off backstage except Dad wouldn't let go of her hand. One more bow.

As we caravanned out of Ridgecrest that night, I sat behind my parents' merged figures. I watched the truck pass beneath a lamppost, lighting the front seat, for an instant revealing Al and the boys squeezed inside, bobbing along shoulder to shoulder, their gazes far from each other. They looked small and overwhelmed by the bulk they hauled, the long white trailer clattering behind them, not even able to turn a corner without Al's slowing down to eye the angles in the side mirror.

A spring rain was falling in the desert. I rolled down the window. The land was alive with singing crickets and wild earth smells I never knew were there. That's how I rode into Barstow—with the night air on my face, feeling hidden things thriving in the dark.

In Barstow we played a high school stage marred by graffiti. "Stacy sucks," "Ray beats off," and "Jenny loves Jesus." Walls, doors, every flat surface stamped with feeble-minded drama. At the vanity, I studied the dark, sooty scrawl carved into the wood and touched a deep, inky hollow expecting pigment to stain my fingers. An onerous narrative screamed at us throughout the night in rotting black epitaphs. "Satan rules," "Eat me." A plethora of body parts, profanity, manifestos—the rant of a demented scribe. Before walking out the stage door that night, my eyes fell on this final declaration, "Wreckers of the World Unite."

The next day, we drove across the flat, airless desert, and soon stalks of dusty quartz broke the horizon. Las Vegas. Through a river of taxis and busses, we inched along the strip, past the rippling and throbbing neon signs of the Frontier, the Riviera, and Caesar's. Somewhere inside those casinos, beyond the slot machines, card tables, and bars, resided the offices of the talent scouts. I found myself scrutinizing the buildings, wondering where their offices were and if they were mean to their secretaries. Each time I imagined them in our audience, they always sat in a rear aisle seat, their faces expressionless, just big masculine jaws and fat pink lips. Strangely enough, they always wore sunglasses, even inside the theater, concealing their unreadable black eyes. In my daydreaming, our magic show was a flickering of storm light across the glass.

At the Flamingo, we scrambled out of the Cadillac, sweaty and fumbling for our bags, with Mom's chiffon scarf blowing in the warm breeze. To the roar of ringing slot machines, we entered the big hotel and dragged ourselves to the front desk and to our little room in a distant tower. That night we went out to meet Mom and Dad's old friends Wayne and Lacy Jackson for dinner on the strip.

A handsome couple arrived, and hugs flew around.

"You kids look like a million bucks!" Dad said.

"Then why do I feel like a nickel?" Lacy Jackson said. Her pink pantsuit sparkled with Valentine's Day glitter.

Someone named The Count would also be joining us. "He's having marital problems," Wayne said glumly. "I think it's contagious."

We scooted into a big booth and drinks were ordered. Lacy dipped one finger into her cocktail glass and tasted it. "Nectar of the lambs," she said, lifting her glass. "No wonder I'm a fan."

"We've got a few shows in town," Wayne said. "Then we do a cruise." He was a bald, paunchy man with a trimmed goatee and a little jack-of-spades lapel pin.

"I told him I wanted to take a cruise and do you know what he does?" Lacy asked us with raised brows. "He books our show on one! I said, 'Wayne, do you understand the word "vacation"?'" She threw her eyes up to the ceiling. "They're all crazy, you can't stop 'em."

A sympathetic comrade was what Mom needed. She touched the base of her neck. "We're on the road again! Just when I thought it was over!" she effused.

They leaned their heads together and Lacy whispered loudly, "Magicians never retire, Helene. They just *pause*." She turned to Dad. "What do you have to say for yourself?"

Dad chomped on a bread stick. "I came, I *sawed*, I conquered."

A big coif of platinum crowned Lacy's head, and her dark, spindly eyelashes came from a box. "When we married, Wayne said I'd be part of his cast of amazing artists. And then I realized I *was* the cast of amazing artists." She patted his back. "Poor Wayne. I help him with his little *tricks*." She rolled her eyes. "He hates it when I call them *tricks*."

Wayne shrugged. "What do I know? I got a tuxedo that weighs twenty pounds."

"Hey, Count!" They beckoned to a man with a long narrow face and droopy eyes. He scooted into our booth.

"Where's Elena?" Mom asked.

"She split, she's gone, left last week," he said, gazing down at his fingers weaved together on the table.

Everyone shook their heads. "Tsk tsk."

He told a tale of three marriages, three divorces.

"Each time, they cited professional magic as the problem," he moaned. "She refused to pick a card anymore."

"Well, honestly, Count," Mom confessed. "I've picked so many I can't remember them."

"Wives put up with it," Wayne said. He pointed his thumb at Lacy. "She thinks she's a glorified busboy."

"Without the tips," Lacy added.

"Elena thought magicians were strange," The Count complained.

Wayne threw his hands in the air. "Don't look at me! My tuxedo is so heavy it stands up by itself!"

Dad talked about our tour. The towns played, turnouts, and future bookings.

"I never had an agent," he told them. "All an agent does is throw down three eight-by-tens of three different people and says, 'Which one do you want?'"

"You gotta have one," Wayne advised. "It's called organized show business. Like the mob."

"Look. No sleeves," Dad said, turning his wrists.

Wayne and Lacy talked of playing nightclubs in Europe in the fifties to escape the onslaught of televisions. "TV sent every road show to an early grave," Wayne said.

Dad remarked casually, "We did okay, we made good money and retired."

My jaw dropped. What did he just say? Then I realized he wanted to impress the Jacksons. "We only left the road because of Cindy," he explained. "We wanted to give her a normal life, put her in school and make a home for her in the suburbs." Wagging a finger at them, he said, "Family always came first."

The words hovered in the air, tempting us to tug them down. I stared at the fanned salami on the antipasto dish. Mom shifted in her seat, trying to rearrange her body to absorb his words better.

I was glad to hear Lacy laugh. "Just another magician giving, giving, giving." Then she leaned across the table and squeezed The Count's hand. "Oh, Count, I *am* sorry about Elena. I'm just in a funk right now. I found out I'm working on my vacation." She shot Wayne a look and said to Mom, "It's not easy being married to a magician. Is it, Helene? We have to make all kinds of compromises."

Even as Mom nodded, I could feel all these unspoken words swarming and colliding inside of her, so many words, too many words, enough to drown in.

Lacy's face softened, and her eyes turned misty. "Sometimes I think of what Wayne and I have done together, all the magic and friends and laughter we've shared. And you know what? I wouldn't change a thing." She squeezed Wayne's arm. "Where would he be without me?"

Mom gave Lacy one of her serene nothing-wrong-here smiles. I found myself doing the same.

Early the next morning, while Mom and I were still in bed, Dad called the casinos. In his green-striped pajamas he sat next to his brief-case with his legs crossed, one pale, narrow foot dangling in the air.

From under the blanket, I watched him take out his yellow list and start to dial.

"I want to talk to someone in charge of hiring talent for the club…I'm Lee Grabel, and I have an illusion show playing tonight. I want someone in the club to see it…What's his name?…Is he in?…When will he be in?…Have him call me. Lee Grabel. At the Flamingo. The show will be at the convention center tonight at eight o'clock. It features a floating piano and vanishing horse."

He jotted something down on his yellow list and moved on to another casino. "I want to talk to someone in charge of hiring talent for the club…I'm Lee Grabel, and I have an illusion show playing tonight. Who can see it?…What's his name? Is he in? Tell him to call the Flamingo."

He kept taking notes and calling casinos. "Tell him my show is in town tonight at the convention center. Let me leave my number at the Flamingo." Another casino: "Lee Grabel at the convention center tonight at eight. Here's my number." And another: "Is he in now?… He's on the phone? Have him call me when he's done. I'm at the Flamingo." He kept dialing until I thought he was done but there was one more. "Yes, I'm Lee Grabel, and I have an illusion show playing tonight. It features a floating piano and vanishing horse. What's his name?…Is he in?…Tell him to call me."

He kept track of the times the secretaries said the casino scouts would be available, and then he called back. "Is Mr. Chilton there yet?…This is Lee Grabel again. Have him call the Flamingo…Is Mr. Jacob available now? When will he be there? Tell him I'm at the Flamingo." Then he dressed in his champagne suit and dashed from the room with his briefcase.

Mom and I lay in bed for a while. Down below, the strip throbbed with people. The motel room still resonated with Dad's voice and his finger in the rotary phone, dialing, dialing. Where was he now? I imagined him scouring those big casinos for the executive offices, talking to secretaries and sitting in big waiting rooms.

We got dressed, watched television, and read. A few hours passed. The phone rang.

Some decisions at first feel so inconsequential. In that split moment they are made, we have no idea of their implications, and the kind of claim they will make on our memory. Forces were stirring that perhaps my mother and I were unaware of.

Certainly, my mother's reason for not answering that phone made sense. "Let it ring," she said. "It could be Dot." We had made loose plans to meet her for breakfast, but Mom was finding Dot's uncompromising nature tiresome and needed a break from her company. A sensible explanation to let a phone ring. We just wanted a little quiet time to putter around and read. Or had my mother and I colluded together, lost heart in this endeavor a long time before?

I can still see us lying around the hotel room with our magazines and books while that phone rang. Our reliability had faltered. We were going to miss our cues. One moment was all it took.

Magic is that fragile; it's that easy.

Even as my father made his rounds to the casinos that morning in his best suit, it was over for us. We let it ring two, three, four times. Then we heard Dad's key scrambling for the lock. He had returned from the casinos, heard the ringing phone through the door, and assumed there was no one in the room to answer it.

The door flew open. Shock registered on his face when he saw us sitting there, letting the phone ring. We recognized our betrayal too late. Mom rushed for the phone, followed by Dad. A club scout calling him back. Mom reached it first. The line was dead.

Dad threw up his hands, his face afire. "Why didn't you answer it?!" he yelled. "I've been calling all morning!"

We were mute. The Sahara, the Stardust, the Sands…which one had we missed?

"We thought it was …" Mom stopped. It sounded so silly. She was aware, as was I, that perhaps her ambivalence had finally gotten the best of her. She had been forced into this tour, and her feelings had finally slipped out of the bags within bags within bags she had tucked them inside of, like so many pieces of bread.

Dad called the front desk, his pen and list ready. "Did anyone just leave a message?" No.

He threw his pen down on the desk and it bounced on the floor. "What do you think I've been trying to do!"

Mom sat in a chair by the window with the desert light flooding in behind her, drowning her out. Dad teetered for a moment on his feet. Maybe he was considering another round of phone calls to the man whose secretary said he was at lunch, or the secretary who said to call back later. Maybe he was thinking about calling the casinos in Laughlin or Stateline. Then his body sagged. He sat down on the edge of the bed and held his head.

I had just been following Mom's lead, or was I? Wasn't it me, of all people, who should have been jumping for that phone? It was possible the magic show needed a love that only its magician could give it. My allegiance had never been pure. I had wanted my father's big dream to win me fans and flattery, to fix my shortcomings. I had hurt others along the way, just as my father had. My craving for grandeur had been a lonely quest. In jumping out of the hat, I was alone in the spotlight.

Being a magician's assistant had never really been my dream. It was fun dressing up and jumping out of that hat, but I didn't have any speaking lines, no starring role, no tricks of my own.

I dropped my head, feeling small and depleted. The hoopla that had consumed me for months drained out of me. Out the window, westward, over the desert and mountains, was Alamo and my bedroom, with my record player and pink hairbrush microphone. As I imagined myself poised before my mirror, my frenzied pretending didn't feel the same. I'd have to find another passion, another fancy thing to love. And maybe it would be as fine and glittery as the magic show.

Our trio went to the casino for lunch, slipping inside a booth under a big Keno screen. A cacophony of bells and coins rumbled around us as we sat there in silence, our eyes shifting around the tabletop to the salt and pepper shakers, the utensils, the napkins. We looked everywhere except at each other.

My parents were tired and in need of good haircuts, naps, and a hot iron to smooth the creases in their clothes, yet the spotlight still radiated from their rumpled figures. Any moment I could hear music, and the whole thing could begin again. All my parents' special charms and wizardry still had a hold on me and would for years to come. They are the dreamy stuff of every hope I have for myself. I've never recovered from them.

Dad exhaled. "You got an ol' ham for a father," he told me.

We raised our heads and smiled.

Time to get to the stage. As we left the casino restaurant, Dad observed the gamblers trying to hit it big and said, "What a bunch of dreamers."

25

VIVA LAS VEGAS!

And now i'll go back to paper debree and data and I'll be just another worker in a whole World of workers. I'll die a cheated women. cheated because something I wanted wasnt Full Filled and i'll realize its just too late.

Lee and Helen at the Academy of
Magical Arts Awards ceremony, 1995

DESPITE OUR HIGH HOPES for Las Vegas, the convention center
did not have a proper stage for us. We were directed to a big empty
room with a low platform at one end. It was called The Golden Room
for the coarse textile weave, the color of a fortune cookie, that covered
every inch of it. The floor, chairs, and even walls were enshrouded in
this sickly dirty-yellow fabric. It was a room for boring conventioneers
or for people pitching kitchen appliances. And we were surrounded
by hundreds of rooms like it at the Las Vegas Convention Center.
Huge empty rooms, some with walls that could be folded in or folded
out to make smaller or larger rooms. We were buried in a catacomb of

vacant, shifting, shuffling rooms. To get to us, our crowd had to walk down three cavernous corridors.

The missed call in the motel room was probably from Dot. At the time, though, I was convinced Mom and I had single-handedly brought down the Broadway Magical Mystery Extravaganza.

That afternoon, sitting silently backstage waiting for showtime, Mom released a long, withering sigh. "I feel so bad."

"Me, too," I said, and that was the last we ever talked of it.

Vegas wasn't our best or worst show. It was a show that had taken us months to learn, hewn from what is left after romance ends— something solid on its feet and predictable in a good way.

During the show, I peeped through the curtain, scanning the crowd for someone who might pass for an agent from the Sahara, the Stardust, the Sands…After our woeful mistake in the hotel room, I had crafted this flimsy and hopeful story: When no one answered the scout's call, the scout decided to see our show and speak to Dad in person. I zeroed in on a man in a gray sports jacket, sitting in an aisle seat. He had a big gold watch and a squinting sternness around his eyes. After the show, watching the man talk to a group of Kiwanis members, I decided he came closer to a high school science teacher than a casino executive.

I joined Mom in the front row and stared at the floor, too numb to think. Not a single talent scout had come to see the Broadway Magical Mystery Extravaganza. Just then, I was convinced that whatever I wanted, whatever wonderful thing I aspired to, would be too much work. And I'd have to be careful. The people I'd ask to help me might let me down, even those I loved. All my big dreams, most likely, would fail. Teacher, bank teller, escrow girl…The implied tedium and failure of these vocations were gone now. Comfort might be found in their manageable demands.

I brought my hand to my face, and there it was again—the smell of the magic show. Suddenly I knew what it was. It was the musty odor of decay. It came from the cloth inside the big top hat and the concave of the levitation table. Each time I emerged from those contraptions, I was anointed with the scent of waste and age. My costumes, skin, and hair all imbued with it. Rotting wood, dank curtains, sour old paint. Even as we breathed love and air into it, the show was being claimed by time.

When the curtains were taken down, I could see Dad undressing behind his wardrobe trunk. He removed his gold medal, unhooked his glittering blue-sapphire vest, and pulled off his bow tie. Unfastening his cuff links, he dropped them in the top drawer, stepped out of his black satin-trimmed trousers, and unbuttoned his white shirt. He arranged them straight and neat on a wire hanger. His slender legs were pale and blue-veined, something excavated from a secret mountain hole.

The crates had been carted off to the idling truck. The boy-movers swarmed the stage for the last items: the cage of doves, hobo luggage, the big gold hoop, and speakers. With the equipment gone, Dad and his wardrobe trunk were the only things left. He changed into his jeans and shirt and sat down behind his trunk. He put his hands up. Pressing his palms hard against his forehead, he dragged them down his face. His hairline sagged, his eye sockets drooped, then his jaw lowered. His palms kept going down, revealing the whites of his eyes. He was trying to erase his face.

Two boy-movers surrounded him with a dolly. He closed up his trunk and let them roll it away.

"Did you even start that article?" Dad asked with irritation, looking up from his yellow list as we finished up the tour in Salinas. Morning light cast a harsh glare across the motel room, igniting his white hair and slashing across his blue eyes that flashed with the question: *what's been going on?*

I don't remember saying no, just feeling stuck in our impasse. He thought the story was onstage, I thought it was backstage.

His promotional packet included photos, letters of recommendation by the sponsors, newspaper reviews, and edited selections of the Napa video. "I wish we could have included your article," he said, sadly. I studied my right hand that had so tightly gripped my pens. I'd done a lot of writing on this tour, none of it for the article he wanted.

He shook his head, implying I had failed in a big way. "Nothing happens unless you make it happen." He figured I was not the kind of girl to make things happen and connect the holy triangle between idea, list, and limb. He also thought Mom had spoiled me beyond repair. Now that he knew, I was relieved. Maybe he'd take me off his yellow list.

I couldn't write about the magic show the way he wanted because I saw it so differently. He wanted to promote the show, while I wanted to surround it with candles, let it grow inside me like a vine with a nocturnal bloom. And when the time was right, I wanted to tell the story of the road my way.

Later that night, on a cold bathroom floor of another motel, I removed my journal from my tote bag and studied it. All that ink made it heavy and imbued it with the import of a historical document. Touching the tirelessly scribed pages, I felt a deep, mysterious satisfaction.

In the next room, in the starched sheets of the bed, I heard my father snoring. Usually, he was too wired from the show for deep sleep. Perhaps with the tour winding down, he could finally rest. He snored with an old man's abandon, long and noisy, and I sensed that he was strangely inconsequential to the night. I reached for a blank piece of paper and started writing. How odd that my father was missing such a big occasion as this, me, writing my first list. When I got back to Alamo, I'd be starting high school, and soon leaving home, beginning my life. There was so much I wanted to do. My hand kept moving, leaving a trail of scratchy blue dreams in its wake. I didn't know if I could accomplish it all, or where it might take me. I just knew I'd keep going even if the help was unreliable, string faulty, and lighting bad.

26

⌒⌒⌒

SHOWTIME

*Bye, Katy. See
yeah. Your my best friend, your alright, even
though you talk to yourself to much.*

Las Vegas headliner Lance Burton before the mural of magicians
from the Royal Dynasty of Magic at The Monte Carlo casino

BACK IN ALAMO, I enjoyed moaning over the lost magic show. I'd
come home from school, complaining about the stupid remarks from
my classmates about my stint in show business. *How do you do that
sawing trick? Did he pull you out of the hat by your ears?*

I daydreamed in class and journaled continuously about the
unfairness of the magic show's demise. Not until I made new friends
sophomore year, did I relinquish the show's exquisite hold on me.
When I joined the high school choir, it was truly humbling to be one
of many voices, second row back, singing songs not cool enough for
my record player. Civil War songs, Broadway songs, Gold Rush songs
and pioneer songs. As I became more occupied with school activities
and adolescent pastimes, my part in the magic show turned into just
a fun story to tell. Years later, I decided my father's return to the stage

was his own unique midlife crisis.

My chronicles of the road ended up filling two big notebooks. I kept these journals on my desk prominently displayed between two ceramic bookends. I loved to open their thick worn covers and marvel at the words I had conjured. Sometimes I showed them to my invisible crowds. "Here are my notes from the tour," I'd tell them, riffling the stacked pages under my thumb. I would feel them behind me, looking over my shoulder, impressed by all my serious documentation in pink and purple pen.

One evening, Cindy came over for dinner and offered to help where Mom could not. Gently pulling me over to the side, she touched my back. "Let me know if you have any questions about boys," she said with a tender smile. I blushed. I had no boyfriend. Still, it was good to know I wasn't on my own.

News about our crew trickled in that first summer back. Clair was hired as an elementary school teacher, and the cousins moved to the Sierra Nevada to become river rafting guides. One morning in July, my father donned his gray suit and walked out the front door, back to his office with his battered briefcase and tan alligator shoes.

Soon after, Al and Dot showed up at the house on their way to Southern California. They gave me a music box in the shape of a white spinet piano. I cranked the little gold knob. A jaunty tune wafted out, a song one of our piano players might have played on their unnatural ascent. Upstairs, I placed the music box on my dresser. No longer did The Floating Piano exist in photos in a box. The magic show's lore and density now belonged to me.

The little white piano had all kinds of secret compartments. The top of the piano opened into a compartment with a mirror, and the keyboard was really a lid to another compartment. The bottom was a drawer with a brass handle. The insides were lined in red felt, and I loved to open and close the little lids and drawers. It was a great place to find and lose things, or lose and find them again.

The following spring, 1978, Dad started formulating again. No drawings of illusions, no dollar signs, no exclamation points. Only his black scribble on his big yellow notepad. One day, he set his typewriter on the dining room table. He was writing a book called *The Life and Illusions of Lee Grabel*. It would be a tribute to his career in magic, with photos, a biography, and the workings of his best effects, including The Floating Piano and his One-Handed Card Production. The table was covered with old photos from the box in the closet. And a few I had never seen before. One was an old black-and-white glossy of an older man with a pointy Van Dyke beard and a stern, piercing gaze. Dante. He looked less friendly than interesting. In another photo, a young, beautiful, dark-haired woman leaned against a Greek pillar, a regal glamour-puss in a long gown.

"Who's that?" I asked Dad. He said Moi-Yo Miller, Dante's leading assistant. Also on the table was a typewritten letter from Dante to Dad. This was *the letter*. The same letter I had heard Dad and Al talking about. It had a fancy orange letterhead that read "Dante the Magician."

"I'm going to include the letter," he told me in an offhanded way. The letter was important then. I examined it closely. He'd taken notes in the margins with his familiar script.

It soon became clear the book was more than his story; it was a declaration of sorts. Long ago, Dad had been chosen by Dante to join a prestigious Royal Dynasty of Magic.

I was to learn the dynasty is a bequeathing, a passing on of stature, title, and audience from one magician to another. It started in 1896, with the untimely death of Alexander Herrmann, the leading magician of the day. With his competition gone, magician Harry Kellar replaced Herrmann in the finest theaters and started to bill himself as the next great magician after Herrmann.

When Kellar retired in 1908, he named Howard Thurston as his successor in a Royal Dynasty of Magic. They even formalized it with a ceremony at Ford's Theatre in Baltimore where Kellar placed a long regal mantle on Thurston's shoulders. In the following years, the tradition continued, with Howard Thurston choosing globetrotting Dante in the 1930s as his heir and Dante naming Dad as his successor in 1954. Apparently, no one knew it. Dante died in 1955 without making a public announcement. I suspect the whole tradition started as an advertising ploy. Kellar took advantage of Herrmann's death to boost his career, and when he chose young Thurston as his "successor," Thurston recognized the publicity such a title would give him. He was even willing to pay Kellar $6,000 for his show equipment.

At the time of Dad's book, the dynasty included these three magicians covering a span of about seventy years, each one representing a different era of entertainment. And they were not even magicians. In the lexicon of magic, they are considered illusionists, which means they fronted their own big theatrical shows featuring flashy productions.

"Dante saw the show in San Fernando," Dad told me. Dante had sat in the audience wearing a straw hat, white suit, and smoking a cigar. He was searching for a young magician to be his successor, and he thought Dad had the talent. "We started talking about me taking over," he recalled.

That was the summer they spent long afternoons at Dante's ranch making plans. He wanted Dad to play his old route through Europe and change his name to Danton, a combination of Dante and Thurston. At the end of the summer, my parents started touring again, and by the following June, Dante was dead of a heart attack. Most folks assumed the dynasty tradition had ended with Dante. Except the letter implied otherwise.

"That's my proof," he told my mother and me. The letter, though, wasn't specific about Dad's claim. There was no such kingly proclamation as *I now pronounce you my successor in the Royal Dynasty of Magic!* Dante and Dad were to combine shows, Dante using his connections in Europe to book my father in the best theaters, but the letter read like two men entering a business transaction. One sentence Dad underlined. "I think we have one target in mind. To create a new up-to-date Master Magician."

"That doesn't prove anything," Mom said sharply, standing over him as he typed.

"It's right there," he said tersely. "In the letter." His eyes never left the keys.

Mom pressed her lips together. "Hmmp."

It wasn't that Mom didn't think he was good enough for such a title or that he didn't deserve it. It was a big announcement, and she knew he would be open to criticism in a public way. My father was an outsider in professional magic. He worked hard and established himself outside the Hollywood clique of magicians, didn't play the big cities, and many magicians just hadn't seen his show. Nor had the popular periodicals of the fifties—*Tops*, *The Sphinx*, and *Hugards's Magic Monthly*—ever mentioned his name. As a matter of fact, there is little recorded history of my father at the peak of his career. He lived on only in old newspaper archives from the small towns of America.

"What are you going to do if no one believes you?" she asked, her voice edged in warning. Bending over so her head was even with his as he typed, she said, "Are you listening? Lee, *listen*." He lifted his chin and continued banging on the keys, ignoring her. Straightening up, she covered her mouth. We knew the signs. His solitary push that excluded everyone else. Nothing would stop him.

"You'll wish you hadn't," she stated, crossing her arms.

"Okay, then." He bristled up from the typewriter. "Arturo and Moi-Yo Montes will vouch for me. They were there." Arturo Montes was Dante's right-hand man and had married Moi-Yo Miller. They were at Dante's ranch during the dynasty talks the summer of 1954.

"You don't know that," she declared and pointed a finger at him. "You don't even know where they are right now."

Soon after, Dad discovered the Monteses lived down the road from us in the town of Santa Clara. He arranged for them to visit the following week.

My father, in a way, did win the fame he wanted. When he declared himself as the successor to Dante in the Royal Dynasty of Magic in 1986, he got a lot of recognition from his peers. Arturo and Moi-Yo Montes were willing to back up his claim, as he had hoped. So began my father's new career in professional magic. He started doing his card and coin routine at magic conventions for The Society of American Magicians and The International Brotherhood of Magicians. He called his new act "A Nostalgic Return to the Golden Age of Magic," and it oozed with affable, gentlemanly charm as he traipsed around the stage, producing cards and coins with a buttery smile. For his finale, he would sit on a stepladder, reminiscing to the crowd about the great dynasty magicians. His last show, at the age of eighty-seven, was the "It's Magic" show in Hollywood at the Kodak Theatre in 2007.

As part of the tradition, my father had to choose his successor in the dynasty. In the early nineties, he started scouting young illusionists, and in 1994 he chose Las Vegas headliner Lance Burton. In a ceremony in Las Vegas, much like Kellar and Thurston had done, Dad placed a mantle on Burton's shoulder to symbolize the passage. My father went on to win the Academy of Magical Arts Masters Fellowship award in 1995. He became a celebrity in some circles of professional magic. Our 1977 tour became a footnote in his career.

Long before that, when Dad first arranged for Arturo and Moi-Yo Montes's visit, we didn't know what awaited my father, who was nearing sixty and often said, "I want to die with my boots on." On the day of their visit in the summer of 1978, Mom prepared a plate of hors d'oeuvres in the kitchen while Dad and I watched the clock. The doorbell rang. Dad flung open the door.

The foursome greeted each other with the fervor of long-lost friends.

After all these years!
You look great.
It's been too long.
What's new in Glocca Morra?

Hugs and kisses flew around the entryway. Mom introduced me. Moi-Yo turned around and, with her hands on her hips, said in her Australian accent, "So you're the rug rat, all grown up now. How do you keep up with these troupers?"

She was dressed in black, a long velvety skirt with one nylon-clad leg exposed. A jacket of dancing sequins shimmered against her white skin. Unusually formal attire for a weekday afternoon, and I wondered if that's all there was in her closet—a night sky of twinkly black house dresses and terry robes of bling.

She was as beautiful as her photo, with her lustrous black hair extravagantly piled on her head. A sleek black-cat quality radiated from her. Together, she and Arturo exemplified cosmopolitan flair.

Arturo's head of thick silvery hair matched his fitted gray suit. He had dark good looks and a reserved manner, and I noted a sliver of an accent from his native Mexico City.

"We brought you a gift in honor of your magical parents," Arturo told me. He handed me two coins in a plastic pouch that read "Scotch and Soda." One was a tawny Mexican centavo and the other a half dollar of muted silver. A magic trick.

"Don't encourage her!" Dad hooted on his way to the ice bucket.

"Champagne! Champagne! Por favor," Moi-Yo chimed in.

Mom looked dumbfounded. She had white and red wine, and all kinds of hooch. She frantically poked about the pantry, returning empty-handed. Dad poured Moi-Yo a white wine. "C'est la vie!" she said, and they raised their glasses. "Cheers! Salud!"

"Merci beaucoup, monsieur!" Moi-Yo said.

"Friends of the Dante show are friends for life," Arturo announced.

We walked out on the patio with appetizers, and everyone sat around sipping their drinks, their chatter replete with the vigor of a Broadway chorus.

Dad asked, "Where have you been all these years?"

They explained that after Dante died, they left professional magic and moved from Southern California to begin a new life in the San Francisco area. Arturo became an engineer at Lockheed Martin, and they settled down with two kids. Moi-Yo became a merchandise purchaser for a department store. Only recently did they start visiting old magic friends.

Moi-Yo gazed away, transported across time. She placed her hand on her chest. "And now I am back in the magic fold." She then brightened up and asked about our recent tour with the magic show. "Did you sell out at the Lido and Wintergarten? Break a leg and all that? When do you load out again?"

Dad dismissed her question with a wave of his hand. "Oh, that tour was just a little tribute to our old show life. A nostalgic return to the road, so to speak." He nodded his head toward me. "We did it for Katy. To show her our old life."

I turned to Dad, my eyes wide. Mom's nothing-wrong-here smile did not falter.

Moi-Yo clapped. "Bravissimo! What a wonderful gift to your beautiful daughter!"

I found myself nodding my head, playing along while I grappled with his defection. He was disowning our beautiful dream and our honorable fight for it, relegating me as an actor in a lie. He smiled broadly as Mom and I looked on, the two witnesses who knew otherwise. He had rewritten the story of his failed comeback tour to suit him, and by the confident tilt of his chin, he appeared to believe it.

I would grow to understand that what made my father great and amazing was also his affliction. He was a smooth omitter and embellisher when it came to his beloved magic show. In the years ahead, he would continue to describe our tour as a sentimental sojourn and an altruistic gesture to me.

Back on the patio, Dad teased, "Besides, we had to go back on the road. For Helene. She insisted on being shot from that cannon one more time!"

Mom gave an uneven grin, and we laughed.

"Let me take a photo of the happy family," Moi-Yo said.

I sat between my parents, enveloped by their tinkling ice, gabardine, and perfume. We exchanged bank-heist smiles. Then Dad turned into a campy comedian, pointing and tickling my waist just as the camera flashed. He raised his glass and toasted Mom and me. "Here's to you, kids!"

Later on, I lay on the bed upstairs, listening to their laughter on the patio. Both couples exchanged hilarious show stories. As their hoots and cackles erupted through our backyard, it occurred to me this could be an auspicious visit for my father. He might get the notoriety he wanted. In this light, our troubled tour across five states resized into something softer and smarter. Maybe it's possible to fail a few times before getting what we want. Maybe mistakes are common along the way—we just can't let them stop us.

I had a slew of favorite pop songs that summer, and as I sang along to my record player, I followed the melody's highs and lows with the ease of a balloon gently bouncing along. *What might seem like the end/ Is something new/ Something just for you.*

In my voice lessons I learned to sing from my belly area, not my throat. I discovered I had an entirely different voice deep within me—pure, clean, and strong. Best of all, I could hit the right notes.

Just then, Mom called me from the bottom of the stairs. "Come on, Kate, we're going to dinner." They were entering the house, a stampeding chorus line, dropping off their clanging glasses and gathering up their jackets in a big noisy fuss

I heard Dad's voice call out, "Let's get this show on the road!" He was rallying the players in a new crusade.

I ran down the hall and leaned over the banister. "I'll stay here."

Holding her purse at the bottom of the stairs, Mom's bright face dampened a little. "Okay, then." She blew me a red kiss. "We'll miss you."

In a whirl of laughter and jokes the front door closed. The house was quiet.

I was nearing sixteen that summer, and eager to drive. With my parents gone, I headed downstairs to the driveway. I opened the door of the Cadillac and slid into the driver's seat. I wanted to leave little Alamo on a grand adventure.

I checked my reflection in the side mirror.

No invisible crowds gazed back at me, only Katy, a young girl with lots of outlandish dreams. I gripped the wheel. I had a show to get to.

EPILOGUE

Twenty years after the tour ended, I went with my parents to empty out the old show trailer which had been stored on a farm near their house. My mother and I watched my father cut the lock with bolt cutters. The doors opened and light flooded in the truck. Mouse scat covered the floor, and the scent of decomposing wood drifted out to us. We began opening crates.

The pink satin ball case housing The Floating Ball *was grossly discolored. It wobbled in my hands, a card castle in a theater draft. The soft black felt that lined the interior of the levitation table had been nibbled away by mice. The cannon barrel's Naugahyde cover had come unglued and fallen away from the metal hoops. The strips of mirror that decorated the barrel now littered the bottom of the crate. Inside the cannon was the wire lady covered in her white sheath, just as we packed her in the last show. I unwrapped her mummy layers, touched her skin of wire stitching, and found her preserved in her chastity.*

From its big green crate, we rolled out the creamy pink piano. Dad removed the board behind the keyboard and we peered inside. Mice had nested in the piano harp and nibbled away the wool felt hammers. The wire strings had popped out, and the sounding board had swelled and cracked from the extreme summer heat in the trailer. I hit a key. Thump. A stone dropped on soft dirt.

Out in the weedy lot in the afternoon light, the entire show appeared to be crumbling. No longer did string, nails, and glue hold the Big Show together. It was now a mess of wire, rhinestones, string, foam, cut glass, vinyl, black felt, chrome, and plywood. Lids did not open; wheels did not roll. Even threads had disintegrated. Silver elastic trim fell away and hems unraveled. Every foulard, drape, and silk had become the bed sheet of mice. The nails and bolts holding the show together could no longer grip the pulpy wood.

From the big gold top hat, I removed the mice-nibbled foulards by two fingers and dropped them in the dirt. Then came the wire cages with the tropical foam birds so decomposed they fell to pieces. Once emptied of its contents, the black felt lining of the hat lay in tatters at the bottom, exposing the ribbed skeleton. Yet the big hat still held its stylish shape and radiated that old-time glitzy razzmatazz. I could imagine some of its raggedy wonder that had so captivated me. Its hard gold exterior was untouched by mice and time, and it gleamed in the afternoon sun like the grit of gone stars.

I remember thinking, somewhere in this lost magic show was a story I had to tell. That young show girl in all her jittery hopefulness wanted to be heard. I was in my thirties when I began writing this book, a project made longer by the fact I didn't want my father to read it because of the tricks I would expose. By the time this is published, my father will be dead.

As part of my research for the book, I reviewed footage from the Napa show several times. Each time I watched my young self jump out of that big top hat, I was surprised by what's so obvious. I was excruciatingly uncomfortable in the spotlight. As I took my bow, the moment appeared ripe with a power I didn't know what to do with. All those watching strangers weren't such a kick after all. In my quick charge offstage, I looked eager to get away, to where I really wanted to be—backstage, with its splintered light and slanted gadgetry. Backstage, where the spotlight never shined and the powers of fortune didn't matter, where my wasted desire dissipated into mist. Backstage was where the real magic happened, everything pulsing under my fingers, where I could just be me in the dim broken light. And I'm still there now, searching for what the magic show meant to me. It's where every daughter of a great magician winds up after her father's show ends. Right here, figuring it out. "You have to hear this. It's wild."

As an adult I've been a newspaper reporter, counselor, property manager, teacher, disk jockey, songwriter...I always figured if I applied my father's tenacity, I could accomplish anything. My stint in the magic show made a big impression. I approached adulthood with the spirit of the open road, moving from city to city, job to job, dream to dream. This is probably why I didn't have children and married late in life. I was always looking for adventure. I've lived in beautiful places, loved and been loved, seen the world, and been blessed with wonderful friends and family. And sometimes, all of it feels as good as jumping out of the top hat.

I now live in New Mexico. In the summer, I watch clouds gather into dramatic thunderheads and the sky darken the way the houselights dim before a show starts. There are so many moments full of unfolding grandeur. I can't wait to discover what comes next.

~THE END

ACKNOWLEDGMENTS

THIS BOOK WOULD HAVE remained just an interesting story to tell without the vision and support of teacher Anne Lowenkoph at Santa Barbara Adult Education. Her enthusiasm inspired me to see myself as a writer and get it down on the page.

David Perez helped me find the story within the story. Much gratitude for his patience and encouragement. Rachel Howard read the manuscript numerous times and instructed me on the nuance of voice. John LaSala brought a little of that New York mojo to the project.

And much appreciation to Judyth Hill and Mary Meade of Wild Rising Press for their editing and design expertise, and most of all for their excitement and belief in this book.

BIBLIOGRAPHY

Kellar, Harry and Temple, Phil and Olson, Robert E. *A Magician's Tour* – Revisited. Publisher, Phil Temple, 2000.

McGill, Ormond. *The Magic and Illusions of Lee Grabel*. Enchantus Productions, 1986.

Olson, Robert E. *The Complete Life of Howard Franklin Thurston Volume 1 and 2*. Calgary, Alberta Canada: Hades Publications Inc. 1993.

Ray, Joel. *We Remember Dante*. Jackson, Mississippi: Northpointe Publishing, 1993.

Photo credit: John LaSala

AUTHOR'S BIOGRAPHY

KATY GRABEL LIVES IN TAOS, NEW MEXICO, where she fits right in as the daughter of the Human Cannonball. A former newspaper reporter, her stories about professional magic have been published in *ZYZYYVA* and *New Millennium Writings*. She shares her time between an old rambling adobe house in Taos with her guitar, fancy dreams and penchant for dancing in her kitchen, and a lovely book-filled casita in San Miguel de Allende in Mexico. She has always seen herself as a magician's assistant, taking notes, and believes daughters of magicians—even more than sons—must make their own way: Daughters must decide whether to be the willing assistant, command the spotlight, or turn away with a story untold. And all will be lost unless we recognize the resiliency and strength of our mothers as they lay down on the sawing table. Yet who can deny, late at night, when the dark is crowded by our failures, that every daughter of a magician must find her own magic.

Fortunate readers of author Katy Grabel's memoir will find the body text aptly set in a modern revival of the iconic font, Adobe Garamond. Garamond is Robert Slimbach's digital interpretation of the original, beautiful, and balanced serif typefaces of the sixteenth-century Parisian engravers Claude Garamond and Robert Granjon.

Slimbach's faithful revival of this font, beloved for how it evokes and improves on calligraphy, is as true in tone to this foundational typeface as this memoir is to Lee Grabel's revival of his celebrated magic show. Adobe Garamond has become one of the essential printing staples since its release in 1989.

Ancient and revered as the art of magic, Garamond is a timeless masterpiece created and re-created by centuries of dedicated craftspeople, and, on a wondrous synchronistic sidenote, all the Harry Potter novels are set in Adobe Garamond.

The titles herein are set in Trajan Adobe, an all-capitals serif typeface created in 1989 by multitalented designer Carol Twombly. Trajan is Twombly's graceful version of classic Roman letterforms adapted from original inscriptions on the base of the Trajan Column, 113 A.D. Another elegant typeface beautifully suited for display work, Trajan is known to have a starring role as a movie poster font. Also, making this typeface a perfect fit for this book, Trajan is said to "exude a sense of strength and authority, instantly evoking a sense of history and tradition." Twombly noted of her work designing typefaces, "I discovered that...placing black shapes on a white page offered a welcome balance between freedom and structure." Certainly, this exacting balance also eloquently describes both the art of magic and the magic we see here in this exquisitely crafted memoir.